AQA Health Social Care

GCSE

Richard Smithson

OXFORD
UNIVERSITY PRESS

rendon Street, Oxford, OX2 6DP, United Kingdom

...iversity Press, is a department of the University of Oxford.
...hers the University's objective of excellence in research, scholarship,
...ducation by publishing worldwide. Oxford is a registered trade mark of
...d University Press in the UK and in certain other countries

Text © Richard Smithson 2009
Original illustrations © Oxford University Press 2009

The moral rights of the authors have been asserted

First published by Nelson Thornes Ltd in 2009
This edition published by Oxford University Press in 2014

All rights reserved. No part of this publication may be reproduced stored in a retrieval system, or transmitted, in any form or by any means, without the prior permission in writing or Oxford University Press, or as expressly permitted by law, by licence or under terms agreed with the appropriate reprographics rights organization. Enquiries concerning reproduction outside the scope of the above should be sent to the Rights Department, Oxford University Press, at the address above

You must not circulate this work in any other form and you must impose this same condition on any acquirer

British Library Cataloguing in Publication Data
Data available

978-1-4085-0398-0

10 9 8 7

Printed in China

Acknowledgements

Cover photograph: Alamy/Sebastian Green
Illustrations: David Banks
Page make-up: Pantek Arts Ltd, Maidstone, Kent

Alamy Avatra Images/1.4D; Angela Hampton Picture Library 2.2C; David Levenson 2.3a; Imagebroker/3.2D; Vario Images GmbH & Co.KG/3.2F, 4.2B, 5.1B; Picture Partners/3.2G, 5.2A; Motoring Picture Library/3.3A; Sally & Richard Greenhill/4.1A, 6.6D; Geophotos/4.1B; Superstock/4.3A; Photofusion Picture Library/5.3A; Photostock- Israel/6.1B; Bubbles Photolibrary/6.2B, 6.7I; Nucleus Medical Art Inc/6.2E; Stephen Bardens/6.2F; Mira/6.2G; Chris Rout/6.3D; Angela Hampton Picture Library/6.4D; A Room with Views/6.7D; Nick Hanna/6.7G; Stock Connection Distribution/6.9B; Janine Wiedel Photolibrary/6.10A;
Keith Morris/6.10E; Oote Boe Photography 3/6.11A; Ashley Cooper/6.11B; Photake Inc/7.2A; Alex Segre/7.2B; Corbis Bettmann/6.1E; Fotolia Cura Photography/3.2A; Alx/6.2D; Galina Barskaya/6.2H; ZTS/6.5B; Yang MingQi/6.5C; Mikhail Tolstoy/6.7B;
Getty Images Iconica/2.2B; Istockphoto 1.1B, 1.2B, 1.2C, 1.2D, 1.3A, 1.3B, 1.4C, 1.6A, 2.1A, 2.3B, 2.4C, 3.1B, 3.2C, 3.2E, 4.3B, 4.4B, 4.4C, 5.1A, 5.1C, 5.2B, 6.1A, 6.2C, 6.3B, 6.3C, 6.4B, 6.4C, 6.8B; Simone Mueller/6.10C; Chris Parker/6.10D; 6.10F; 7.1A; PA Photos John Birdsall/2.4B; David Davis/4.4A; 6.5D; Department for Transport/6.7H; Photofusion Janine Wiedel/1.6C; Rex Features Burger/Phanie/4.2A; Alix/Phanie/4.2C; 5.3B; Samaritans 4.1C; Science and Society Picture Library 6.1F; Science Photo Library Sotiris Zafeiris/5.1D; BSIP, Raguet H/5.1E; AJ Photo/5.2A; 6.1C; Dr Kari Lounatmaa/6.1D; LA LA/6.6B; David Nicholls/6.6C; Samuel Ashfield/6.7C; Coneyl Jay/6.7F; Lea Paterson/6.8C; Joseph Nettis/6.9A; Tom McHugh/6.11B. With thanks to
Sue Sharp for photograph research.

Although we have made every effort to trace and contact all copyright holders before publication this has not been possible in all cases. If notified, the publishers will rectify any errors or omissions at the earliest opportunity.

Links to third party websites are provided by Oxford in good faith and for information only, Oxford disclaims any responsibility for the materials contained in any third party website referenced in this work.

Contents

Introduction 4

UNIT ONE

1 Human development 8
1.1 Life stages and types of development 8
1.2 Development in infancy 10
1.3 Development in childhood 14
1.4 Development in adolescence 16
1.5 Development in adulthood 20
1.6 Development in later adulthood 24
Human development practice questions 26

2 Coping with life events 28
2.1 Life events 28
2.2 Sources of support 32
2.3 Relationships 36
2.4 Effects of neglect, abuse and lack of support 38
Coping with life events practice questions 40

3 Influencing factors 42
3.1 Factors affecting self-concept 42
3.2 Factors affecting development 45
3.3 Effects of factors in a person's life 53
3.4 How factors inter-relate 55
Influencing factors practice questions 56

UNIT TWO

4 Needs and services 58
4.1 Introduction to Unit 2 58
4.2 Access to services and barriers to access 62
4.3 Services – needs, aims and care actions 64
4.4 Researching Assignment 1 66

5 Job roles and skills 66
5.1 Skills of care workers 68
5.2 Principles of care and codes of practice 74
5.3 Researching Assignment 2 76

UNIT THREE

6 The nature of health and wellbeing 78
6.1 Definitions of health and wellbeing 78
6.2 Factors affecting health – regular exercise 82
6.3 Factors affecting health – diet 88
6.4 Factors affecting health – substance misuse 92
6.5 Factors affecting health – unprotected sex 96
6.6 Factors affecting health – genetically inherited diseases 100
6.7 Factors affecting health – preventing illness and managing risk 104
6.8 Factors affecting health – lack of personal hygiene 112
6.9 Factors affecting health – economic factors 114
6.10 Factors affecting health – social factors 117
6.11 Factors affecting health – environmental factors 122
The nature of health and wellbeing practice questions 126

UNIT FOUR

7 Health measures and health plans 128
7.1 Planning and researching Assignment 1 128
7.2 Planning and researching Assignment 2 130

Index 132

Introduction

■ How to use this book

This book covers the information you need for your course.

Learning Objectives

At the beginning of each section or topic you'll find a list of Learning Objectives based on the requirements of the specification, so you can make sure you are covering the information you need to know for the exam.

Objectives
First objective.
Second objective.

Study tips

Don't forget to look at the Study tips throughout the book to help you with your study and prepare for your exam.

Study tip
Don't forget to look at the Study tips throughout the book to help you with your studies.

Practice questions

These offer opportunities to practise doing questions in the style that you may encounter in your exam so that you can be fully prepared on the day.

AQA examination questions are reproduced by permission of the Assessment and Qualifications Alliance.

Visit www.oxfordsecondary.co.uk for more information.

AQA GCSE Health and Social Care

■ Meet the neighbours

In this book you will be able to follow the lives of a group of neighbours who live in Ramsay MacDonald Street. Understanding the things that happen to them will help you learn about health and social care.

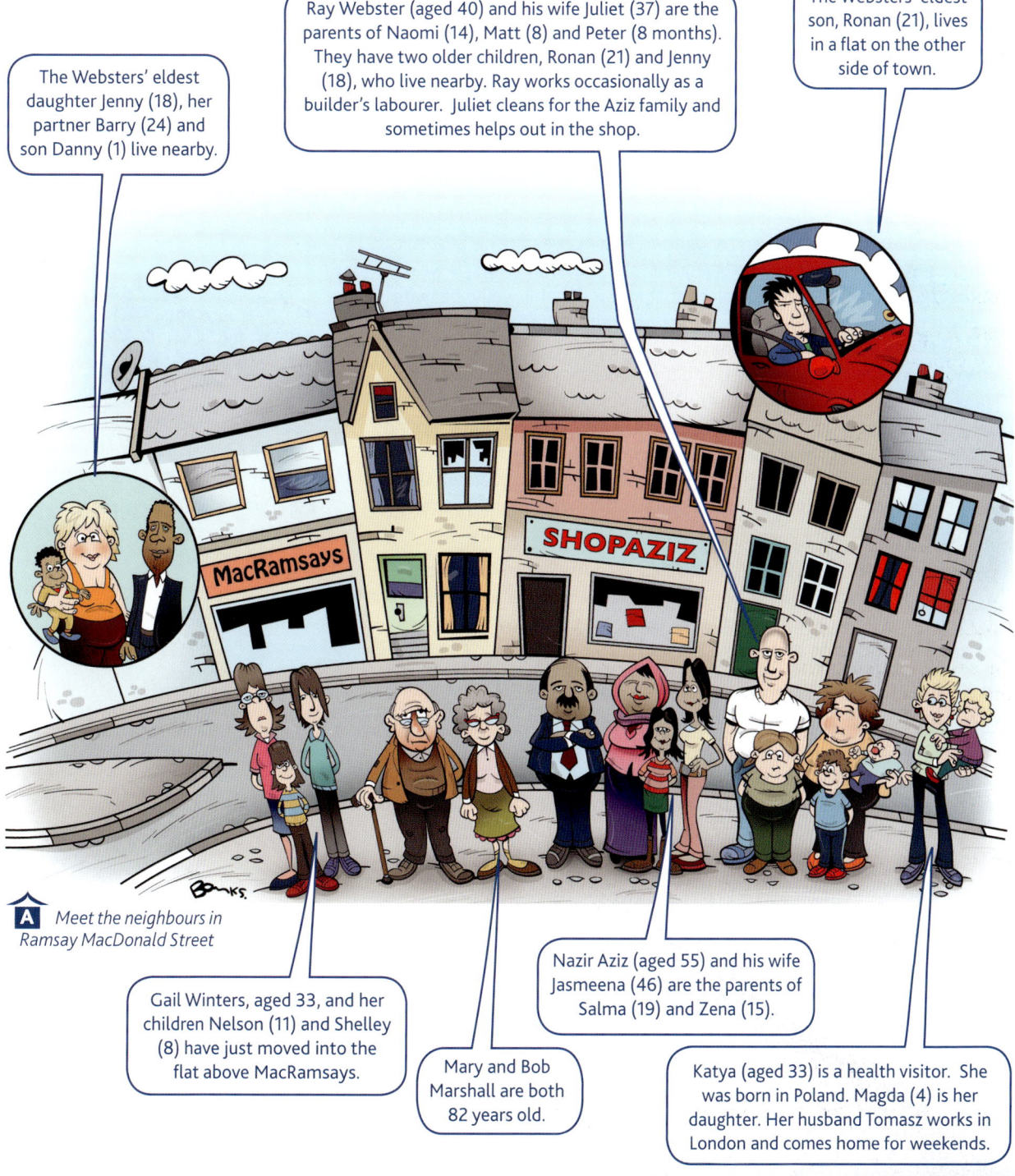

Meet the neighbours in Ramsay MacDonald Street

The Websters' eldest daughter Jenny (18), her partner Barry (24) and son Danny (1) live nearby.

Ray Webster (aged 40) and his wife Juliet (37) are the parents of Naomi (14), Matt (8) and Peter (8 months). They have two older children, Ronan (21) and Jenny (18), who live nearby. Ray works occasionally as a builder's labourer. Juliet cleans for the Aziz family and sometimes helps out in the shop.

The Websters' eldest son, Ronan (21), lives in a flat on the other side of town.

Gail Winters, aged 33, and her children Nelson (11) and Shelley (8) have just moved into the flat above MacRamsays.

Mary and Bob Marshall are both 82 years old.

Nazir Aziz (aged 55) and his wife Jasmeena (46) are the parents of Salma (19) and Zena (15).

Katya (aged 33) is a health visitor. She was born in Poland. Magda (4) is her daughter. Her husband Tomasz works in London and comes home for weekends.

6 Introduction

Meanwhile...

... in Ramsay MacDonald Street ...

Mary and Bob Marshall are just getting ready to go shopping in the street market, when Bob complains of feeling a bit strange. He looks pale and sweaty.

'Have you got a pain?' asks Mary.

'Arm hurts a bit,' Bob replies.

'Well, what have you done to it?' asks his wife.

'Nothing.'

'If you don't want to go shopping, why don't you just say so? You don't have to think of excuses,' snaps Mary as she leaves the house.

Meanwhile the Aziz family is not at home. It is a special occasion, and they have left Juliet Webster in charge of the shop. They have just arrived in Cambridge, where Salma is going to study for a degree in chemical engineering. She is the first person in the family to go to university. Nazir parks the estate car in the street outside Salma's college. There are lots of other families, bringing sons and daughters. Nazir is wearing his best suit and tie. Jasmeena is wearing her best green silk and a hat. Salma is wearing a black skirt and white blouse. Her mother insisted that it would be quite wrong for her to wear her usual jeans and tee shirt. Salma thinks she looks like a waitress. Nazir and Jasmeena are surprised to see that most of the other parents are casually dressed and the students are mostly wearing jeans. Some of them are quite scruffy. Nazir wonders whether this famous university is all it is cracked up to be. Zena just looks at everything around her. She has never seen such beautiful buildings, or such interesting-looking people. The whole family has to make several trips, carrying Salma's things up to her room. Jasmeena bursts into tears as they wave goodbye to Salma and set off back home.

When they arrive home, there is an ambulance outside the shop. Katya is walking Mary Marshall from the ambulance to her house. Mary is crying and muttering to herself: 'He said he was ill, but I didn't take any notice. I should have called the doctor, shouldn't I? Now what am I going to do?'

At the hospital, Bob Marshall's body is already in the mortuary.

Later that evening, Ronan Webster and four of his friends are drinking at a country pub 10 miles out of town. At closing time they argue about which of them was supposed to drive them home. Because of a misunderstanding, they have each drunk over eight units of alcohol. They decide to draw lots to decide who will drive. Ronan's name is picked out. Fortunately, the country road is quiet and Ronan drives carefully. There are some temporary traffic lights on a bend. Ronan keeps going. His friends shout at him to stop, but Ronan just says, 'What's the problem? The light's green.'

B *Find out what happens next in Chapter 1*

Guidance for teachers

Chapters 1, 2 and 3 prepare students for the Unit 1 examination. These chapters include:

- the information students need to learn
- activities
- examination questions
- tips on tackling examination questions.

Chapters 4 and 5 give guidance for researching the Unit 2 assignments.

Chapter 6 prepares students for the Unit 3 examination. Activities, tests and questions are like those for Unit 1. There are no past papers for this unit.

Chapter 7 gives guidance for planning and researching the Unit 4 assignments. Most of the factual information needed for this unit is already covered in Chapter 6.

Key terms are highlighted in blue in the text and are defined when necessary. These are words that candidates should use in examinations.

Activity

Most of the activities can be done either as group discussions or as individual work. Some of them are based on incidents from the lives of the Ramsay MacDonald Street neighbours. These 'neighbours' are included partly to make this book more appealing to students and also to help them relate the syllabus content to the real world.

The events that happen to the neighbours are not intended to imply any judgements about people of any social or ethnic group, or about people of different sexes and sexuality. Events are included in order to illustrate themes and content in the specifications.

links

These highlight websites or weblinks that students might find useful.

Practice questions

These can be answered in class or set as homework.

Learning workout

These give students practice before trying to answer questions.

Teachers should also consult the AQA Specifications and Teachers's Guide for this subject. Note that there is some information in this textbook that is not given in the specification, but might occur in examination questions, for example, questions about Huntington's disease.

> **Study tip**
> The tips give specific guidance to students on common pitfalls. They also direct students to Practice questions at the end of each chapter that will test their knowledge and understanding.

1 Human development

1.1 Life stages and types of development

Life stages

A person's life can be divided up into a series of life stages:

- **Infancy** This stage is from birth to three years. A person in this stage is an infant.
- **Childhood** This stage is from four to 10 years. A person in this stage is a child.
- **Adolescence** This stage is from 11 to 18 years. A person in this stage is an adolescent.
- **Adulthood** This stage is from 19 to 65 years. A person in this stage is an adult.
- **Later adulthood** This stage is from 65 years onwards. A person in this stage is sometimes called an older person or an elderly person.

Types of development

Development is about how a person grows, increases in ability or improves. One example is how a person's body grows and changes during adolescence. Another example is an infant starting off being able to feed by sucking and then gradually moving on to eating solid foods with a spoon.

Human development can be divided up into the four types described below.

Physical development

Physical development includes **growth**, which means an increase in a person's size, and **motor development**, which means becoming able to make movements.

The usual way of measuring a person's growth is to measure their height at different ages. Parents often measure their children's height during childhood. You can also measure growth by weighing a person at different ages. This gives a measure of mass or weight. This measure of growth is most often used for infants, and also in adulthood.

Motor development is sometimes divided up into two sorts:

- As **fine motor skills** develop, the child becomes able to make precise movements using just a few muscle groups. Holding a pencil is one example.
- As **gross motor skills** develop, the child becomes able to make whole-body movements, using large muscles and muscle groups. Dancing is one example.

Mobility is the ability to move yourself about, such as by crawling, walking or running.

> **Objectives**
>
> Know the names and ages of the five life stages.
>
> Describe gross and fine motor development.
>
> Describe physical, intellectual, emotional and social development (PIES).

> **Activities**
>
> 1. What are you like? Before reading any further, write at least five sentences describing yourself. You might like to compare what you wrote with what someone else writes about you. Do they see you in the same way as you see yourself?
>
> 2. Draw up a chart with five columns – one for each of the five life stages. Look at the description of the neighbours who live in Ramsay Macdonald Street (see Introduction, page 5). Write each name in the appropriate column.

Motor milestones are important stages in motor development, such as being able to walk.

Intellectual development

This means developing thinking abilities. It includes:

- getting better at remembering things
- becoming able to understand language and to speak
- getting better at solving problems, like making everyday life decisions
- learning basic ideas – sometimes called **concepts**. Being able to count things is an example of using number concepts.

Emotional development

Emotional development involves developing positive and negative feelings about everyday situations, as well as becoming able to express and to control these feelings. Positive feelings include joy, interest, excitement and satisfaction. Negative feelings include anger, fear, sadness, disgust and hatred.

Emotional development also includes development of the **self-concept**. A person's self-concept is the beliefs they have about themselves. Self-concept includes **self-esteem** – a person's beliefs about their own value.

What you wrote in Activity 1 will give a snapshot of your self-concept. You might have included basic facts about your name, age and where you live, what you can and cannot do, what activities you enjoy, and your beliefs.

Social development

This means developing the skills and routines that enable people to get along with each other. These skills include **communication**, **cooperation**, sharing, turn-taking, **leadership** and tolerance. A person with good social skills is able to make **relationships** with other people, and is likely to have a wide circle of friends. Meeting and communicating with other people are **social interactions**.

Social development starts in the family. As children grow up they make relationships with other people.

Summary table for revision

B Key words about development

Physical	Intellectual	Emotional	Social
■ Growth, measured by height and weight ■ Gross motor skills ■ Fine motor skills	■ Learning ■ Language ■ Thinking ■ Problem solving ■ Memory	■ Developing positive and negative feelings ■ Learning how to express feelings ■ Learning how to control feelings ■ Developing the self-concept – including self-esteem	■ Making relationships ■ Social skills ■ Social interaction ■ Having a wide circle of friends

Study tip

Who learnt all the PIES?

You will find the names of these four types of development very useful in the exam. Remember **P**hysical **I**ntellectual, **E**motional and **S**ocial by the first letter of each word.

A Social interactions are important

links

For more on communication, see Chapter 5, Job roles and skills, page 69; for more on relationships, see Chapter 2, Coping with life events, page 28.

Learning workout

Look at this list of 16 words to do with development. Sort the words into four groups, under the four headings: 'Physical development', 'Intellectual development', 'Emotional development' and 'Social development'.

friendships	feelings
memory	sharing
speech	walking
growth	concepts
anger	height
leadership	learning
sadness	motor skills
self-concept	cooperation

1.2 Development in infancy

Meanwhile... in Ramsay MacDonald Street ...

Katya is going to give her four-year-old daughter a bath. Magda does not like having a bath. Even before the taps are turned on she starts screaming at her mother. Katya knows how to deal with Magda's tantrums.

A

Objectives

Explain physical, intellectual, emotional and social development in infancy.

Activities

1. What should Katya do:
   a. Let Magda go without a bath on this occasion?
   b. Make an excuse to leave the room, then come back when Magda has calmed down?
   c. Give her a good hard smack?
   d. An alternative action suggested by you.
2. Think about the advantages and disadvantages of each choice. To find out what Katya actually did, look ahead to Chapter 6, The nature of health and wellbeing, page 112.

■ Physical development

Growth

Infants grow very fast. The infant goes from around 50 cm in height at birth to around 75 cm at one year. Weight increases even more quickly, from around 3 kg at birth to around 8 kg at one year. **Milk teeth** start to appear from the age of six months. These are teeth that fall out during childhood, to be replaced by permanent, adult teeth.

Motor development

At birth, infants cannot make many movements. During infancy, motor development is very fast.

B *Development milestones*

Average age	Gross motor milestones	Fine motor milestones
6 months	Rolls over, can sit if supported	Reaches out for objects, passes objects from one hand to the other, puts objects to mouth
9 months	Crawls, sits without help, pulls up to a standing position, stands while holding on to furniture	Pokes objects with a finger, picks things up using finger and thumb
1 year	Stands without help, walks if helped	Drops objects on purpose, points to things
15 months	Walks without help, crawls upstairs	Picks up small objects with a pincer grip
18 months	Climbs on to chairs, walks upstairs	Scribbles, turns pages of books
2 years	Runs, kicks a ball	Turns door knobs, eats with a spoon
3 years	Can dress and undress, rides a tricycle, stands on one foot	Threads small beads, uses a pencil gripped between thumb and first two fingers

> **Activities**
>
> 3 An infant is developing normally. She can walk and run, turn the pages of a book and open doors. When she draws, she holds the pencil in her fist. About what age is she?
>
> 4 A little boy is 12 months old. He can walk and tries to crawl upstairs. He can pick up small blocks with the first finger and thumb of one hand. Is the boy's development typical, a bit ahead or a bit behind the typical?
>
> 5 You have been asked to test the fine motor development of a three-year-old. Suggest some simple pieces of equipment you could use.

> **Study tip**
>
> If you are asked a question about an infant's gross motor skills at, for example, one year, you can include **all** the motor skills up to and including that age. So you could answer with rolling over, sitting, crawling and standing without help.

Intellectual development

Infancy is the life stage in which the most important learning takes place. The infant learns, but without being taught. Some of this learning comes from copying other people. For example, infants learn the language that they hear spoken.

Language skills that are gained during infancy include:

- being able to name objects
- speaking short sentences
- asking questions
- understanding what other people say
- following simple commands.

Thinking skills that are gained include:

- colour concepts – being able to recognise colours
- number concepts – being able to count
- shape concepts – being able to recognise simple shapes.

Towards the end of this stage, infants can also understand simple rules and they develop some memory for events.

C *Starting to crawl is a gross motor milestone*

Emotional development

Emotions

Infants show positive and negative emotions from birth. They express emotions by crying when in distress, for example when in pain or tired, and screaming when frustrated, for example when hungry. At about six weeks old, infants start to smile at faces. Later they show pleasure, for example when being tickled or in face-to-face contact with a parent.

From around two years old, infants often have **tantrums**. This shows that an infant is developing the expression of emotions but is not yet able to control this. A parent who gets angry with an infant having a tantrum usually makes things worse. The best way to help an infant get out of a tantrum is to keep calm. You can either distract the infant or move some distance away.

D *Infants learn colour concepts through play*

Self-concept

Self-concept begins to develop during infancy. At 18 months, most infants can recognise pictures of themselves. Later in infancy, self-concept includes basic factual information such as whether the infant is a boy or a girl.

Attachment

The most important event in an infant's emotional development is the development of **attachment**. This happens when the infant is between around seven months to one year old. An infant's first attachment is with someone they see very often, usually a parent. The infant shows a dislike of being separated from the person they are attached to. If an attached infant is separated, even for a short time, they might become very distressed, crying and unable to be comforted by anyone else. The infant tries to stay as close as possible to the person they are attached to. The infant follows the person around and clings to them. At this time, the infant also begins to show a fear of strangers. Over the next few months, the infant also attaches to other familiar people, for example grandparents and older brothers or sisters.

E *An attached infant tries to stay as close as possible to a parent*

The word '**bonding**' is sometimes used to mean attachment. Some infants do not show very strong attachment. This sometimes happens when the parent neglects the infant, or is not sensitive to their needs. In this situation, someone might say that the infant 'has not bonded well'.

An infant is more likely to explore and play when together with the person they are attached to. Being together seems to give the infant **self-confidence** or a feeling of safety. At around three years old, some infants can put up with short separations from people they are attached to. This means they can go to a nursery school or a crèche.

■ Social development

During the first few weeks of life, infants seem to prefer to look at faces, or pictures of faces, rather than at other things. This is the beginning of social development. At around six weeks, infants often smile at faces. When attached, infants show a fear of separation. During this stage, infants usually play by themselves, as long as a familiar person is not far away. Towards the end of this stage, infants begin to show some interest in other children.

Summary table for revision

F *Development in infancy*

Physical development		Intellectual development	Emotional development	Social development
Growth	Motor			
■ Increase in height ■ Increase in weight ■ Milk teeth	■ Crawls, sits, walks, climbs, runs ■ Pokes objects, points to things, picks up and drops objects ■ Pincer grip	■ Language, names of objects, sentences, understanding speech ■ Concepts of colour, shape, number	■ Crying and screaming ■ Self-concept ■ Attachment ■ Tantrums	■ Smiling ■ Attachment

Chapter 1   Human development   13

... in Ramsay MacDonald Street ...

It's Monday morning. Katya is visiting her next-door neighbour, Juliet Webster. It's not a social call. It is part of Katya's job as a health visitor. She has come to check up on the development of Peter, Juliet's youngest child. Every child should have a developmental assessment when between six and nine months old. Peter is nine months old. It's not going to be easy for Katya, because the room is full of people. As well as Juliet and Peter there is Juliet's daughter Jenny and her one-year-old son Danny. Matt, Juliet's eight-year-old, is there too. Juliet and Jenny stub out their cigarettes when Katya arrives.

'Not at school today, Matt?' asks Katya. Matt grins at her. 'He's got a bit of a tummy ache today,' says Juliet. While Katya chats to Juliet, she watches Peter playing. She knows that he was born prematurely and had a low birth weight, so his development has to be carefully monitored. She notices that he rolls about on the floor but does not try to crawl. At one point, she holds out a toy to him and he smiles at her and reaches for it. Then she sits Peter up and holds him in position by his arms. He seems a bit wobbly in that position and cannot sit up on his own. Then Katya asks Juliet to mute the television, while she checks Peter's hearing. While Peter is looking at his mother, Katya rings a bell to one side of him. He turns to look at the bell.

Jenny says she is a bit worried about her little boy Danny. She says that Danny has started to be very clingy, and cries when she leaves him alone. She is worried that if she keeps picking him up when he cries, he will be spoiled or 'grow up to be a wimp'. Katya explains that most infants get clingy at that age. Letting him stay close to her and picking him up when he wants will make him feel safe. Trying to avoid him when he is clingy will make him clingy for much longer, she explains. Juliet looks at her daughter. 'I could have told you that, love,' she says.

By now, Matt is feeling a bit neglected. He dances into the middle of the room like a gorilla and shouts to Katya, 'I'm not a wimp. I can jump off the high board at the pool, me.' Just then his father enters the room, unshaven and wearing only tracksuit bottoms. Matt ducks behind the settee.

Activities

6   Identify three things Katya did to check Peter's development.

7   Is Peter's motor development normal?

8   Why has Danny started to be clingy?

9   Identify one feature of Peter's social development.

10 As a health visitor, Katya noticed some other things that might affect the health and wellbeing of members of the Webster family. What did you notice?

Learning workout

1   Infants can learn colour concepts by playing with blocks of different colours. Suggest two other concepts that can be learnt in infancy.

2   At what age do infants:
a   start to attach?
b   most often have tantrums?
c   start to smile?
d   first stand without help?

Study tip

Try practice question 1 at the end of this chapter (page 26).

1.3 Development in childhood

■ Physical development

Growth

During this stage, children continue to grow in height and weight at a fairly slow and steady rate. Their milk teeth begin to fall out at around six years old, and are replaced with a complete set of **permanent teeth** by around 12 years. Bladder and bowel control is fully gained during this stage.

Gross motor development

Children develop better coordination and mobility skills, such as jumping, hopping and riding a bicycle. Strength increases, and **stamina**, which is the ability to use strength over a long period, increases too.

Fine motor development

Control of small movements increases. The child can draw recognisable pictures, for example of people. The child can catch a ball and use household tools like tin-openers and screwdrivers.

> **Objectives**
> Explain physical, intellectual, emotional and social development in childhood.

A *Milk teeth begin to fall out at around six years old*

■ Intellectual development

A key feature of intellectual development in childhood is **curiosity**: children typically want to know about things; they like factual information, for example about dinosaurs. They also like stories. Young children learn a lot through play.

Language development continues. The child's **vocabulary** increases. This means that they get to know thousands of different words. The child can say and understand more complicated sentences. The child learns to read and write.

B *Children can learn rules and strategies for games*

The child's problem-solving skills increase, including being able to do simple arithmetic. For example, the child can work out how much change should be left out of £1 after buying some sweets.

The child's ability to learn increases. They can learn the rules of sports and board games and can work out winning strategies in computer and console games. The child can also see other people's points of view. The child's memory for events develops. For example, a child will be able to remember what presents she got on her last birthday.

Earlier memories are usually of sensations like smell, taste, sound and vision. Later memories feature more recall of what people said. Most people do not remember events occurring before the age of around three years. This probably means that memory for events does not develop until childhood.

> **Activity**
> Try to remember five events that you experienced at different times during childhood. For each event you remember, try to decide what age you were at the time. Write down a few details about each event, or describe each event to a friend. Don't include 'second-hand' memories, such as things you did or said that parents have told you about.

Chapter 1   Human development   15

Emotional development

During this stage, children get better at controlling their expressions of emotion. For example, they have fewer tantrums. They can sometimes hide their emotions from others. Young children who hurt themselves (for example by tripping over a step) are able to choose whether or not to cry. Older children are better at expressing emotions in words.

Children are also able to put up with short separations from parents, for example when they go to school. This means that the child is developing **autonomy** – the ability to control their own actions and to show more **independence** (not rely so much on others).

Also during this stage children develop some sensitivity to the feelings of others, for example noticing when a parent is angry. They also begin to develop **empathy**, the ability to share the feelings of others. For example, they might feel sad when a friend is upset. Children also begin to choose between people and objects that they like or dislike.

During childhood, self-concept is often based on abilities or actions the child can perform. For example, an eight-year-old girl is asked to describe herself. She starts off with the usual factual information about name, age and sex. Then she says that she is good at football, can cook samosas, ride a bicycle and swim. Her self-concept includes what she thinks about her abilities.

C   Self-concept in childhood

Social development

Early in childhood, new social skills develop. These include the ability to share, take turns and cooperate. For example, children learn to queue for a turn on a slide and to play family roles in games in the house corner of a day nursery.

During this stage, parents are still the most important people in the child's social world. For example, a child is most likely to talk to a parent about something that is worrying them. Attachment, although weaker is still quite noticeable, particularly when the child is ill or tired. Young children enjoy being held or cuddled.

In early childhood, friendships start to develop. Children begin to have special or preferred friends, especially at primary school. These friendships can quickly change and usually do not last long.

> **Study tip**
>
> Try practice question 2 at the end of this chapter (page 26).

Summary table for revision

D   *Development in childhood*

Physical	Intellectual	Emotional	Social
■ Grows in height ■ Increases weight ■ Permanent teeth ■ Increasing strength, stamina and coordination ■ Hops, rides bicycle ■ Draws pictures, uses tools	■ Learns through play ■ Language – larger vocabulary, complex sentences ■ Reading and writing ■ Problem solving – arithmetic ■ Memory for events	■ Control of emotions ■ Empathy ■ Has likes and dislikes ■ Tolerates short separations ■ Self-concept includes abilities	■ New social skills – sharing, turn-taking, cooperation ■ Relies on parents for support ■ Attachment weaker ■ First friendships

1.4 Development in adolescence

Objectives
Describe physical, intellectual, emotional and social development in adolescence.

Meanwhile... in Ramsay MacDonald Street ...

Zena Aziz, Naomi Webster and Nelson Winters walk to school together. It is Nelson's first term at secondary school. He is a bit embarrassed by having to walk with the older girls. Once they are out of sight of the street, he will walk some way behind them. Zena has been asked to 'look after' him by Nelson's mum. Naomi asks him if he has got a girlfriend yet. Nelson is even more embarrassed. He says that all the girls in his class are bigger than him, and some of them are 'enormous'.

A

Zena thinks that this is not very tactful, because Naomi is quite large herself. As Nelson falls behind, Zena wonders whether she ought to say anything to Naomi about body odour. Zena's mother often tells her that she should not 'meddle' in other people's affairs, but Zena thinks her mother is wrong about this. She often disagrees with her mother. This morning there was an argument because Jasmeena noticed that Zena was wearing eye make-up and told her to remove it. Sometimes Zena feels very fond of her mother, and sometimes she feels really angry with her. Usually she manages to hide her anger.

■ Physical development

Growth

Two important aspects of growth during adolescence are the **adolescent growth spurt** and **puberty**. The adolescent growth spurt is a time of very fast growth, especially in height. In girls, this starts at around 10 years old and peaks at around 12 years old. In boys, the growth spurt takes place around two or three years later. Growth of muscles follows on later. Some adolescents start the growth spurt earlier and some later. Growth of the arms and legs is rapid, and adolescents quickly outgrow their clothes. In girls, the hips become broader; boys show greater muscle development than girls and their shoulders become broader.

Puberty means becoming sexually mature, that is able to reproduce. It is the result of growth linked to the increased production of body chemicals called **sex hormones**. These include **oestrogen** and **progesterone**, which are present more in girls than boys, and **testosterone**, which is present more in boys than girls.

In girls, this process results in the growth of breasts, an increase in the size of the vagina, the start of **menstruation** ('periods') and the

Study tip

The TOP-SECRET method for revising

Write down short notes on the information you want to learn. Read it a few times, then put it aside and try to write it all down from memory. Then compare what you wrote with the original page, and re-learn the bits you missed out. Keep doing this until you can recall perfectly. Practise this with the summary tables in this chapter.

beginning of **ovulation** (the production and release of eggs). In boys, the results include an increase in the size of the testes; deepening (breaking) of the voice; an increase in the size of the penis and the ability of the penis to become erect; the production of sperm; and later the growth of hair on the face. Both boys and girls also grow pubic hair and armpit hair. Armpit hair increases the risk of body odour, so adolescents might have to improve their hygiene practices.

Most of the growth leading up to puberty is to do with developing the ability to reproduce.

The development of pubic hair, breasts in females and a deep voice and facial hair in males does not directly contribute to reproduction. These features are called **secondary sexual characteristics**.

Summary table for revision

B *Growth in adolescence*

	Girls	Boys
Growth spurt	10–12 years	12–15 years
Puberty	■ Increase in size of vagina ■ Menstruation ■ Ovulation	■ Increase in size of testes ■ Increase in size of penis ■ Erection ■ Sperm production
Secondary sexual characteristics	■ Breasts develop ■ Pubic hair	■ Facial hair ■ Voice breaking ■ Pubic hair

C *Highly technical gross motor skills can be developed during adolescence*

Motor development

Adolescents usually increase their strength, stamina, coordination and motor skills, particularly if they practise. For example, highly technical gross motor skills can be developed in activities such as dance, mountain biking, rock climbing, surfing and skateboarding.

Technical fine motor skills, such as those used in drawing, hairdressing or playing a musical instrument, also develop.

Intellectual development

Problem-solving skills develop to include solving hypothetical problems, such as algebra in mathematics. The ability to concentrate increases. Language skills continue to improve, such as the ability to organise information to give long answers to questions in speech or in writing.

Learning continues during adolescence, and strategies for memorising information are used. Adolescents tend to learn more ways or strategies for learning, particularly if they practise. Some adolescents lose the curiosity or desire to learn they had as children.

D *Some adolescents lose the curiosity or desire to learn they had as children*

Emotional development

Remember that, in childhood, self-concept included:

- basic factual information such as age and sex
- information about actions and abilities.

An adolescent's self-concept also includes beliefs that might be political and religious. Examples are strong beliefs about animal welfare or global warming.

Body image becomes a more important part of the self-concept in adolescence. This is partly because of the growth that occurs around puberty. A person's body image is the beliefs that the person has about their own body shape and size. When a person's body image is very different from what people think is an ideal body shape and size, this can reduce self-confidence and self-esteem.

Self-consciousness develops during adolescence. This means that adolescents begin to think about what other people might be thinking of them. This can be very embarrassing. As a result, blushing and shyness can be a problem for some people.

Adolescents sometimes seem to over-react to situations. They get more angry, excited or upset than the circumstances warrant. These emotional over-reactions, which happen partly because of the actions in the brain of body chemicals including hormones, are called '**mood swings**'.

E *Most adolescents are strongly influenced by their peers*

Adolescents gradually rely less on parents for emotional support and instead rely more on friends. Attachment to parents is reduced, so that most adolescents are quite happy to spend time away from home. Autonomy (or independence) increases, as adolescents become more and more able to make their own decisions, form opinions of their own and look after themselves. This can lead to a dislike of being controlled by other people. This is shown when adolescents disagree with and challenge authority figures such as parents and teachers.

Even so, most adolescents do not show complete autonomy. Some of them are strongly influenced by their **peers**. Peers are usually people of the same age, for example attending the same school. As a result of puberty, most adolescents have powerful sexual feelings. This often results in strong feelings of attraction to possible sexual partners.

Social development

Although social skills increase during this stage, adolescents can still experience **social awkwardness**. For example, adolescents can upset or offend other people unintentionally and can misjudge situations. This might be partly because of a lack of ability to see the likely effects of their actions on other people.

During this stage, friendships with peers become deeper and longer lasting. Compared with friendships made at primary school, friendships made during adolescence last much longer, often a lifetime. Adolescents are likely to talk about their feelings or things they are worried about to friends rather than to parents.

During adolescence, people usually increase their circle of friends. This is partly because secondary schools are usually larger than primary schools. It also happens because adolescents tend to rely less on their parents for guidance and support; they are more influenced by their peers. Also during this stage, adolescents are likely to join groups or clubs based on some shared interest, like sport, recreation or music.

Following puberty, adolescents develop relationships with people – girlfriends and boyfriends – because of sexual attraction. Although often intense, these **romantic relationships** are typically quite brief.

Summary table for revision

F *Development in adolescence*

Physical	Intellectual	Emotional	Social
■ Growth spurt ■ Puberty – sexual maturity, secondary sex characteristics ■ Increased strength, stamina, coordination	■ Hypothetical problem solving ■ Increased concentration span ■ Increased language skills ■ More learning strategies	■ Body image important ■ Self-consciousness ■ Mood swings ■ Sexual attraction ■ Greater autonomy	■ Deeper, stronger friendships ■ Greater peer influence ■ Less parental influence ■ Social awkwardness, ■ Relationships based on sexual attractiveness

Activity

1. Now re-read the description of the three adolescents walking to school (page 16).
   a. Nelson is of average height for boys his age. Why are all the girls in his class bigger than him?
   b. Pick out examples of social and emotional development typical of adolescents.
   c. Naomi has not changed her hygiene routine recently, but now she has a problem with body odour. Why?

Study tip

Try practice question 3 at the end of this chapter (page 26).

1.5 Development in adulthood

■ Physical development

Growth

Adults don't increase in height, although they can gain weight, usually because of an increase in body fat. In some more active adults, weight gain is the result of continuing muscle growth. Eyesight gets poorer, and more people need glasses at this stage. Some men lose hair from the scalp during adulthood. Towards the end of this stage, hair on the head usually starts to turn grey.

The menopause

Towards the end of adulthood – usually between around 45 to 55 years – the **menopause** occurs in women. The menopause means the end of a woman's ability to conceive a child. The woman produces no more eggs – stops ovulating, stops menstruating and is infertile. Some women also have side effects known as '**hot flushes**', which are sudden increases of temperature lasting for around five minutes. Some women have **night sweats** which can disturb sleep. Other effects that sometimes occur round the time of menopause are mood swings and headaches. These side effects happen because of a change in the production of sex hormones. The woman's body produces less oestrogen and progesterone.

Men become less fertile as they get older. They produce fewer sperm that can fertilise an egg. Unlike in women, there is no sudden end to fertility. There is no 'male menopause'. Some men in adulthood lose the ability to have erections (this is known as **impotence**). Some men lose sexual motivation, or lose sexual interest in their partners. Men who are overweight, drink too much alcohol or smoke heavily are much more likely to become impotent.

Motor development

Early in adulthood there is often an increase in strength, stamina and coordination. However, from around 30 years old, these features decline. Motor skills used in more everyday situations, including **work** (employment), are fairly well maintained throughout adulthood in people who stay healthy. Towards the end of adulthood, the joints become less flexible – they feel stiffer.

■ Intellectual development

Many adults learn relatively little compared with children; they also lose their curiosity, so intellectual skills tend not to increase. There are, however, exceptions, such as young adults who continue to study, for example at university; also some people, for example scientists, still have a childlike curiosity right through adulthood.

> **Objectives**
> Explain physical, intellectual, emotional and social development in adulthood.

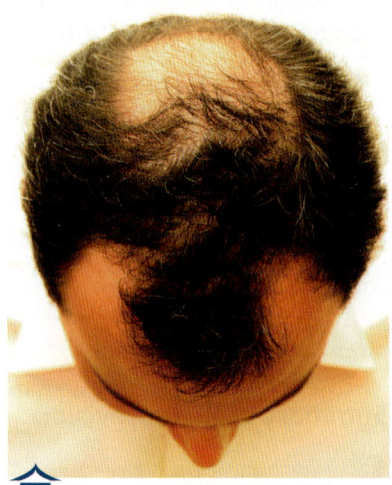

A *Some men start to lose hair from their scalp during adulthood*

What does increase through adulthood is practical knowledge and experience of situations and events. This can enable adults to make more sensible decisions and judgements than less experienced adolescents and children. (This experience built up over the years is sometimes called **wisdom**.) Even so, some people act unwisely right through adulthood.

Emotional development

Self-concept continues to develop, with a person's family, work and achievements forming important features of this. Adults become less self-conscious than adolescents and gain confidence with experience. Concern with body image is usually less than in adolescence, especially in adults who are in long-term, stable relationships.

B *Some adults continue to study*

Adults are usually more emotionally stable than adolescents and are better able to control feelings.

Social development

Early adulthood is a time when many people form long-term partnerships. These are usually based on a sexual relationship. One type of partnership is marriage. Also early in adulthood, a lot of people have children, and develop some of the skills needed to look after them. Very soon after an infant is born, and sometimes before, parents usually develop a strong bond with the infant. This bond means that parents love the infant and have a strong urge to protect it. This parent–infant bonding is quite different from the infant's attachment to a parent, which happens towards the end of the first year of life.

C *Many adults develop relationships with work colleagues*

Many adults develop relationships with other people at work. These working relationships are sometimes also friendships. With experience, social skills, such as leadership, increase.

Summary table for revision

D *Development in adulthood*

Physical	Intellectual	Emotional	Social
■ Peak strength, stamina, coordination ■ Weight gain ■ Menopause (women) – end of ovulation and menstruation, hot flushes	■ Reduced curiosity ■ Increase in knowledge ■ Practical experience, wisdom	■ Self-concept includes family, work, achievements ■ Increased confidence ■ Emotionally more stable	■ Long-term partnerships ■ Bonding with infants ■ Work relationships ■ Increased social skills, e.g. leadership

Meanwhile...

... in Ramsay MacDonald Street ...

It's Monday evening. Zena is in the kitchen with her mother and grandmother. 'Have you no homework to do now?' asks her mother. Zena shakes her head. 'Well, as you have nothing to do you can take these cakes next door to Mrs Marshall. Cheer her up a bit. Go on now.' Zena can tell that her mother wants her out of the way. She guesses that the two women are going to have a serious talk about something.

E

Zena has been leaning on the doorbell for about two minutes when Mrs Marshall opens it. 'Who is it?' she asks, even though she knows Zena very well. 'It's me. I've brought you some cakes,' says Zena. 'I wasn't expecting anybody,' says Mrs Marshall. 'Nobody visits nowadays. Anyway, it's nice to see you.'

Mrs Marshall makes them both a cup of tea. This takes time, because she has to find her glasses first. 'I used to keep forgetting where I put them,' she says. 'So now I always keep them in that cupboard, but they aren't there.' Zena helps her to look for the glasses and eventually finds them in the microwave oven, which is just underneath the cupboard. There is always a funny smell in the house, and Zena is surprised that Mrs Marshall doesn't do something about it.

When the tea is made, they sit down in the front room. Zena tells Mrs Marshall about the letter she received from her sister at university. Mrs Marshall tells Zena about all her aches and pains. 'I can't get into the bath any more, I'm so stiff. My teeth are going wobbly and my hair's falling out. I'm neither use nor ornament. Take my advice, and don't live to be old.'

Chapter 1 Human development 23

This makes Zena smile to herself. She asks, 'So, at what age should I kill myself?' Mrs Marshall is shocked at this talk of suicide in one so young and makes Zena promise never to think of ending her own life. She threatens to tell Jasmeena. 'No, please don't tell Mum. She'll kill me!' says Zena, dramatically. Mrs Marshall notices the look in Zena's eyes and they both start laughing. They each have one of the cakes. 'That's nice,' says Mrs Marshall. 'Ginger, is it?' 'No,' says Zena, 'it's cinnamon.'

Next door, Jasmeena is having a talk with her mother. Jasmeena has reached the menopause. 'It's a relief in some ways, to think no more periods,' she says, 'but I keep going hot and cold. And I think I sometimes get a bit more cross than I ought to with Zena and Nazir.'

F

Jasmeena's mother seems to read her daughter's mind. 'And how is the master of the house treating you these days. Is he patient?' 'Yes, Nazir is very good. He is caring,' says Jasmeena. 'You are worried that, if you neglect him, he will have sex with some other woman, is that it?' asks Jasmeena's mother. 'You must make sure that you keep on with things in the bedroom. It's good for you. You will find it gets better again. Some of my friends used to say they had the best sex of their lives after they'd got over the change. Just make sure he keeps fit, and don't let him eat too much.'

Activity
Identify symptoms of the menopause in the discussions between Jasmeena and her mother.

Study tip
Try practice question 4 at the end of this chapter (page 27).

1.6 Development in later adulthood

Physical development

Growth

Growth does not occur in later adulthood. People in this stage get shorter as the discs in the spine thin and dry out. Bones become more brittle, and falls are more likely to result in broken bones. Weight usually reduces late in this stage, mainly because of loss of muscle and fat.

Blood pressure increases, and so does the risk of **strokes** (leakage of blood in the brain) and **heart disease**. The **immune system** does not work so well. This means that older people are more likely to get infections. The skin becomes thinner and less elastic. Wrinkles develop and, in light-skinned people, small brown patches sometimes called 'liver spots'. Small knocks are more likely to result in bruising.

The hair becomes thinner and turns white. There is usually some loss of teeth, even in those whose teeth remained healthy during adulthood. Also very common is some loss of hearing, especially for higher-pitched sounds. Eyesight changes too, with most individuals becoming long sighted, i.e. only able to focus at a distance. The senses of taste and smell are also reduced.

Older people also have to urinate more often than younger people.

Motor development

During this stage, there is loss rather than development of motor skills. Reduced strength, stamina and **flexibility** (ability to bend easily) mean that people are weaker and less agile. Reduced mobility, such as having difficulty in walking, is quite common. **Reaction times** are longer (i.e. reactions are slower). These changes mean that older people are more likely to trip or fall.

Intellectual development

In most people in this stage there is little or no intellectual development. Instead there is a loss of thinking, problem solving, language skills and memory. Thinking becomes less flexible. This means that people in later adulthood find it hard to adapt to new situations and ideas.

People in this stage can be slow in thought, lose a train of thought, or forget words and names. They also make **action slips** such as pouring tea into the milk jug. There is some loss of short-term and long-term memory. People with very severe memory loss tend to remember only things from many years before. This sort of memory loss happens to people with Alzheimer's disease.

> **Objectives**
> Explain physical, intellectual, emotional and social development in later adulthood.

A Older people develop wrinkles

B People in later adulthood are more likely to make action slips

However, in the early years of this stage, following **retirement** (i.e. stopping work, usually because of age) some people do continue to learn and take up new interests. Activities that require problem solving, such as crossword puzzles and board games, can reduce or delay intellectual decline. Even better is the opportunity to continue working. People who do this are able to use the wisdom they have built up throughout adulthood.

☎ Emotional development

Retirement can result in a person feeling less valued than before and wondering what purpose their life can serve. For some people, the job they do is an important part of their self-concept, so retirement will be a loss. This might also bring reduced self-esteem. During this stage, the decline in abilities can result in a loss of confidence, especially if people have difficulty in caring for themselves.

For some people in this life stage, there is continued companionship in a long-term partnership and continued enjoyment of a sexual relationship. However, the death of a partner is also very likely during this stage, and this **bereavement** can be very upsetting. After the end of a long-term relationship the person might not be able to form another partnership and so might become isolated and lonely.

☎ Social development

In this final life stage, it is common for a person's social circle to get smaller. For example, retirement means less contact with workmates. Later in the stage, social contacts might be reduced by the death of friends or a partner.

Reduced mobility and increased weakness often mean that the person leaves home less often. This can lead to **social isolation**. This in turn leads to a loss of social skills, for example increased selfishness, so that social contacts are less satisfactory and friendships harder to make.

Services such as luncheon clubs and day centres can help to reduce isolation and help people form new friendships.

Activities

1. Now re-read the description of Zena's visit to Mrs Marshall (page 22). Pick out examples of the physical, intellectual, emotional and social effects of ageing on Mrs Marshall.

2. Re-read the description of Jasmeena's conversation with her mother (page 23). What aspect of intellectual development in older adulthood is suggested by the fact that she asks her mother for advice?

Study tip

Try practice questions 5 and 6 (page 27).

C *Day centres can help to reduce isolation*

Summary table for revision

D *Development in later adulthood*

Physical	Intellectual	Emotional	Social
■ Getting shorter	■ Forgetting words	■ Reduced self-concept	■ Less social contact
■ Weight loss	■ Action slips	■ Reduced confidence	■ Retirement
■ Skin thinner, less elastic	■ Slower problem solving	■ Reduced self-esteem	■ Death of partner
■ Reduced hearing, eyesight	■ Slow to adapt to new ideas	■ Upsetting bereavement	■ Social isolation
■ Reduced strength, stamina, flexibility, agility	■ Reduced short- and long-term memory	■ Loneliness	■ Reduced social skills
	■ Reduced memory for recent events		

Practice questions

1. **(a)** Describe the development of mobility in infancy. Give the age at which each milestone is reached. *(5 marks)*

   (b) Give **two** examples of intellectual development in infancy. *(4 marks)*

   (c) Give **two** examples of social development in infancy. *(4 marks)*

2. **(a)** Explain **two** ways in which children are different in social development compared with infants. *(6 marks)*

   (b) Outline **three** examples of intellectual development that happen during childhood. *(6 marks)*

3. **(a)** **(i)** Give **one** secondary sexual characteristic that occurs in males and females. *(1 mark)*
   (ii) Give **two** secondary sexual characteristics that occur in males but not females. *(2 marks)*

   (b) Explain how physical development leading up to puberty is caused. *(3 marks)*

   (c) Outline **three** features of social development in adolescence. *(6 marks)*

   (d) Explain why adolescents are usually more self-conscious than children. *(5 marks)*

4   **(a)** Describe how self-concept changes from infancy to adulthood. *(5 marks)*

       (b) Outline **three** ways in which adults develop physically, apart from the menopause. *(6 marks)*

5   Ameka has reached the menopause.

       (a)   **(i)** In which life stage does the menopause occur? *(1 mark)*
              (ii) Describe the physical changes Ameka will experience during the menopause. *(3 marks)*

       (b) Explain the likely effects of the menopause on Ameka's emotional development. *(5 marks)*

AQA, January 2005

6   **(a)**   **(i)** Give **two** reasons to explain why people in later adulthood might become socially isolated. *(4 marks)*
              (ii) Suggest **two** ways in which the social isolation of older people can be reduced. *(2 marks)*

       (b) Explain why older people are more at risk of breaking bones than adults are. *(4 marks)*

2 Coping with life events

2.1 Life events

Types of life event

Everybody experiences a range of events during life, and these can affect our development. Some of these **life events** are expected, such as puberty or retirement. Others are unexpected, such as having an accident. Life events are associated with three types of changes:

- physical changes
- relationship changes
- changes in life circumstances.

Objectives

Explain physical changes in life.

Explain relationship changes in life.

Explain changes in life circumstances.

Distinguish between expected and unexpected life events.

Explain the effects of life events on development.

Physical changes

Physical changes are changes to your body. These include things like puberty, having an injury, developing an illness and (in women) the menopause.

Relationship changes

Relationship changes include making new relationships and the ending of existing ones. Examples of making new relationships include making friends at a new school, starting a relationship with a girlfriend or boyfriend, starting to live with a partner, getting married, gaining a new sibling (i.e. a brother or sister) and having a child of your own. Examples of the ending of existing relationships include splitting up with a friend or partner, divorce and the death of friends or relatives.

Changes in life circumstances

Changes in life circumstances include starting or leaving school or college; moving house; getting a new job; retirement; and losing a job, because of being dismissed or being no longer required (**redundancy**) or because temporary employment has ended.

Expected and unexpected life events

Some of the life events outlined above are expected – they happen to many or most people and can be predicted. Others are unexpected and less predictable.

A *The death of a relative is a major cause of relationship change*

B Life events

Expected life events	Unexpected life events
- Starting school - Puberty - Leaving school - Getting a job - Leaving home - Getting married - Having children - Moving house - The menopause - Retiring	- Having an accident - Being a victim of crime - Illness - Becoming disabled - Separation or divorce - Being made redundant - Death of a relative (bereavement)

Effects of life events on development

Life events can have some positive effects and some negative effects on a person. Sometimes the effects are quite large; sometimes they are small. When thinking about the effects of life events on a person, you should remember the four areas of development (PIES).

Let's look at an example from Ramsay MacDonald Street. You might remember that Jenny Webster and her partner Barry had a son, Danny, about a year ago. Both Jenny and Barry were surprised at what a big difference Danny made to their lives. Here are the effects on Jenny:

- **Physical** Jenny did not get much sleep during the first six months of Danny's life. He kept waking up in the night, and she kept on having to get up to feed him and change his nappy. Jenny put on a little weight because she was too tired to be very active and had started to eat more.
- **Intellectual** Jenny learned quite a lot about caring for an infant.
- **Emotional** Jenny felt a strong bond with Danny as soon as he was born. Being a mother is an important part of her self-concept. She was anxious at first because Danny was quite ill to start with. She also began to feel annoyed with Barry, because he did not do much to help look after Danny. She argued with Barry because they were having sex much less often than they did before Danny was born, because she felt so tired. The arguments made her depressed. She comforted herself by eating more.
- **Social** Jenny has a new relationship – with Danny. He is the person she is with most often. Jenny's relationship with Barry is weaker, because he often goes out without her. Jenny does not go out in the evening with her friends so often. Jenny is spending more time with her mother Juliet. They get on better now and take it in turns to look after Danny and Peter (Juliet's infant son).

C

Now think about this from Barry's point of view. He used to have a strong relationship with Jenny, in which sex was important for both of them. Now that there is another person in the family, Barry is getting much less attention from Jenny. She seems to care more about the baby than she does about him. She does not often show affection to him. Barry used to think that babies and children had to fit in with what their parents wanted. It seems to Barry that Danny is taking over their lives. Barry does not think a baby should have that much influence. These effects on Barry are mainly emotional and social.

Activities

1. Remember that effects can be positive or negative, and big or small. Draw up a table with the four PIES down the left-hand side and 'Positive' and 'Negative' along the top. Fill in the table, using the description of the effects on Jenny of Danny's birth. Put any positive effects in the 'Positive' column and say whether the effect is big or small. Do the same with negative effects in the 'Negative' column.

	Positive	Negative
Physical	None	Lack of sleep – big effect
		Weight gain – small effect

2. Think how you were affected by starting at a new school. Try to think of at least one effect under each of the PIES headings. Which effects were positive and which were negative? Which was the biggest or most important effect on you?

3. Every new member in a family has a big effect on relationships. It can change each person's influence or importance within the family. Think of a family consisting of a mother and two children. How might they be affected if the mother takes a new partner?

4. Now think about how Matt Webster might have been affected when his younger brother Peter was born.

5. List the effects on Salma's life of going to university. Use PIES.

6. Do the same for Ronan's car accident.

7. List all the life events that have happened to the Ramsay MacDonald Street neighbours so far. Which were expected and which were unexpected?

8. Try to decide how Jasmeena might have felt when her daughter Salma left home to go to university. What difference might this make to Jasmeena's life?

Chapter 2 Coping with life events 31

… in Ramsay MacDonald Street …

Ronan Webster has been in hospital since his accident. He can't remember anything about it, but one of his friends told him that he drove through a red light and hit another car. Ronan does not look badly injured, but he has some brain damage. Following brain surgery, he cannot speak, but he can understand speech. One side of his face droops down. He can stand up but cannot yet walk. He gets upset when friends and workmates visit him, because they tell him about the things they have been doing and that he cannot do himself. His girlfriend does not visit very often, and, when she does, she avoids looking at him most of the time. He feels useless and hates having to rely on people to do everything for him.

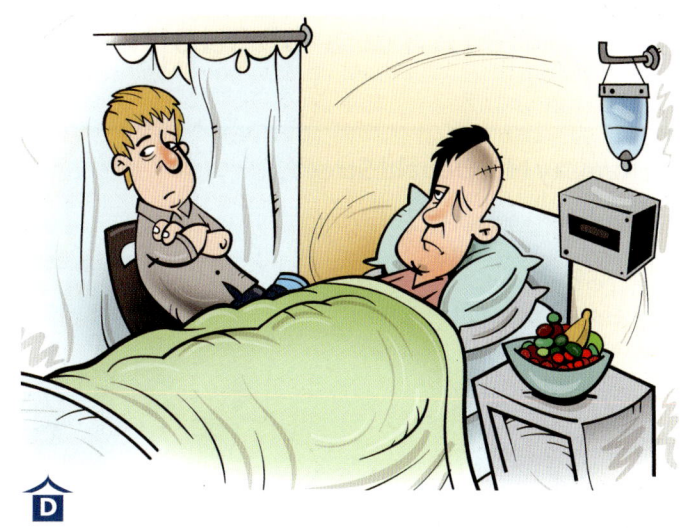

D

It is a month since Salma went to university. As she watched the rest of her family drive away that day, Salma felt lonely and a bit anxious, although she didn't show it. In the next few weeks, a lot of things happened. She started to play badminton again with a girl who lived in one of the rooms along her corridor. She made friends with people from different parts of Britain and from several other countries too. Her first impression was that everyone else knew much more than she did. She bought a second-hand bicycle to get to lectures on the other side of the town. She was surprised at how good the food was in her college and began eating more than she used to at home. Within three weeks she had a boyfriend, who was from France. He seemed to know more about Britain than she did. Salma enjoys some of the engineering lectures but has had to learn a lot of new mathematical methods quite quickly.

Activity

9 Using card of one colour, make a set of 15 cards. On each card write 'Life events' in small letters and one of the words/phrases in the list below in large letters.

puberty	getting married	moving house
starting work	gaining a sibling	menopause
getting cancer	redundancy	breaking a leg
retirement	getting divorced	starting school
bereavement	getting pregnant	making new friends

a Now sort these cards out into three sets – one set of **physical changes**, one set of **relationship changes** and one set of **changes in life circumstances**.

b Then shuffle the cards together and sort them out again, this time into two sets, one for **expected events** and one for **unexpected events**.

Study tip
Try practice questions 1 and 2 at the end of the chapter (page 40).

2.2 Sources of support

Objectives
Explain types of sources of support.

Identify ways of helping.

Meanwhile... in Ramsay MacDonald Street ...

Mary Marshall is very upset. She has had a letter saying that her pension payments will be less. She does not really understand the letter. Her late husband, Bob, used to deal with their financial affairs.

Mary has stopped eating regular meals, because she doesn't see the point of cooking just for one person. When she makes a pot of tea she often puts out two cups, forgetting that her husband is no longer there. She does not go shopping very often, just next door to buy a packet of biscuits every now and then. As Mary sits looking at the letter, Juliet enters the room. 'The keys were in the door, so I let myself in,' she says. 'You forgot to pick up your change when you were in the shop just now. Here you go.' Juliet notices that a gas ring is still burning on the cooker and turns it off.

A

Life events often cause problems for people. This is sometimes because they lead to a change in routine. People have to adapt to changes caused by life events. A person who starts work for the first time might have to adapt to getting up earlier in the morning. They might also have to adapt to working with different people. This is when sources of support can be helpful. There are three types of sources of support:

- partners, family and friends
- **professional carers** and services provided, for example, by local authorities and the National Health Service (NHS)
- **voluntary services** (these are not run by government and do not make profits) and **faith-based services** (these are provided by or connected with local religious organisations).

Partners, family and friends

A person's partner, family members and friends can often give useful support, because they know the person well. This kind of support is sometimes called **informal support**.

An important part of a parent's role is to provide support for their children. This can include washing and dressing them, treating minor illnesses and injuries, giving advice and guidance and providing emotional support.

Friends often give each other emotional support. Neighbours sometimes give each other practical support. This support might include shopping, looking after children and helping out with transport.

B *Parents support children by treating minor injuries and by giving emotional support*

Professional carers and services

Examples are given in the table below; the people listed provide **formal support**.

C *Examples of how selected professional carers can help*

Professional carers	How they help
General practitioners (GPs)	Diagnose and treat illnesses, e.g. prescribe painkillers
Occupational therapists	Advise disabled people on aids and adaptations in the home
Physiotherapists	Provide **exercises** (physical activities) to help people recover movement in limbs after illness or injury, and also treat pain in joints
Community (or district) nurses	Visit people in their own homes to give advice and treatment, e.g. changing wound dressings
Social workers	Carry out needs assessment for people who need help in coping. Support and protect families in crisis and support individuals who are at risk of harm, such as children
Home care assistants	Help people in residential homes with personal care, including washing, and dressing
Health care assistants	Provide personal care for hospital patients

Voluntary and faith-based services

The following are examples of voluntary organisations:

- **Citizens Advice Bureau**, which gives advice, guidance and information about money matters, legal problems and housing.
- **Relate**, which tries to help couples whose relationships are in difficulty (Relate can sometimes help to prevent divorce).
- **Age Concern**, which provides practical help for elderly people, including day centres and personal care at home.

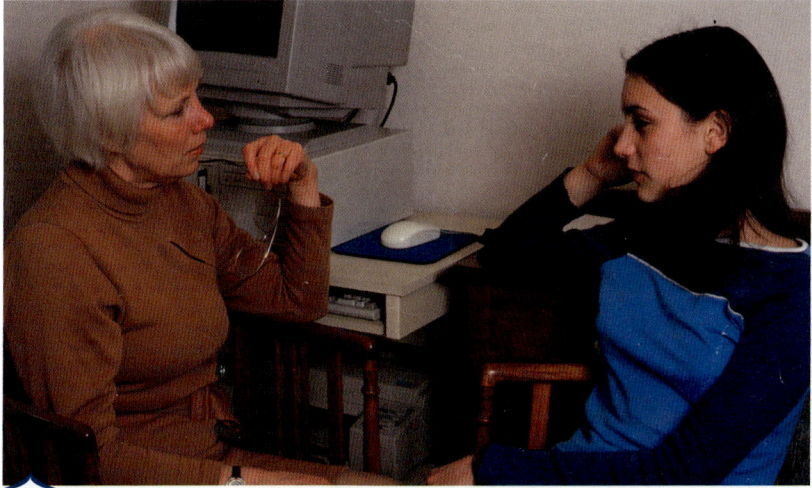

D *Life events can cause problems for people and advice, guidance and information can help*

- **Samaritans**, which provides a **counselling** and listening telephone service for people who are extremely distressed and might be considering suicide.
- **ChildLine**, which is a telephone helpline for children who are at risk of abuse, including bullying and self-harm.

Faith-based services are provided by or connected with local churches, chapels, mosques, temples and synagogues.

The three sources of support can help in several ways.

E *Examples of different ways of helping*

Way of helping	Source of support	Example
Providing treatment	Physiotherapist	Helping an old person with exercises to enable them to walk again
Providing protection	Social worker	Taking an abused child into care
Giving everyday help	Neighbour	Shopping for an elderly person
Giving guidance or advice	Citizens Advice Bureau volunteer	Helping a person who has been made redundant to manage their debts
Giving information	Parent	Explaining about menstruation to a girl before puberty
Counselling	Relate counsellor	Trying to help a couple through a problem in their relationship
Listening – emotional support	Partner	Getting the person to talk about the difficulties they are having in a new job
Spending time with the person	Friend	Visiting a person in hospital

Activities

1. Draw up a table like the one above, with the eight ways of helping in the left-hand column. In the middle column, write the name or the job title of a person who has helped you in the ways listed on the left. In the 'example' column, write what they did to support you.
2. Salma Aziz and Mary Marshall have both had to adapt to recent life events. Which one of them seems to be adapting more easily? Think of reasons why there is a difference in how well they are adapting.
3. Which of the neighbours have provided Mary with informal support so far?
4. Suggest one type of professional carer who could provide Mary with support, and suggest how they might be able to help.
5. Do the same for one voluntary organisation.

Learning workout

Exercise 1
Look at the examples of support listed below:
1. A father asks his daughter what she did at school, and lets her talk about her day.
2. A son helps his elderly mother to clean her house.
3. A couple discuss their relationship problems with a Relate worker.
4. A GP prescribes painkillers.

For each example, decide whether it is an example of:
- providing treatment
- providing protection
- giving everyday help
- giving guidance or advice
- giving information
- counselling
- listening
- spending time with a person.

Exercise 2
Dougal has been injured in an accident at work. He has been discharged from hospital but has pain and weakness in one arm. He is unable to work and is worried about getting into debt.

1. Suggest one voluntary organisation that might be able to support Dougal, and suggest how it could help.
   (Hint: look for clues in the description of Dougal, and use one of the 'ways of helping' listed in Exercise 1 in your answer.)
2. Suggest one professional care worker who might be able to support Dougal, and suggest how this worker could help.
3. Suggest two different ways Dougal's workmates could provide him with informal support.

Exercise 3
Sheila is 85 years old and lives alone. A neighbour sometimes does some shopping for her. Her priest visits her to chat and find out how she is. A social worker visits to find out whether she needs extra help. Every Thursday, Sheila goes to the local Age Concern day centre.

From the description above, identify:
1. a voluntary service
2. an example of informal support
3. a faith-based service
4. a professional carer.

> **Study tip**
> Try practice question 3 at the end of this chapter (page 40).

2.3 Relationships

There are several types of relationship including:

- family relationships
- friendships
- intimate personal and sexual relationships
- working relationships.

> **Objectives**
> Identify types of relationship.
> Explain how relationships affect development.

A *Examples of relationships*

Type of relationship	Examples
Family relationships	Parent–child relationships and **sibling** relationships (siblings are children within the same family)
Friendships	Friendships with **peers** (peers are people who are equals in some way, e.g. children of the same age)
Intimate personal and sexual relationships	Typically between partners, boyfriends and girlfriends
Working relationships	Relationships between a teacher and a student; a GP and a patient; an **employer** and an **employee**; and relationships with other work colleagues (work **colleagues** of the same status are also called peers)

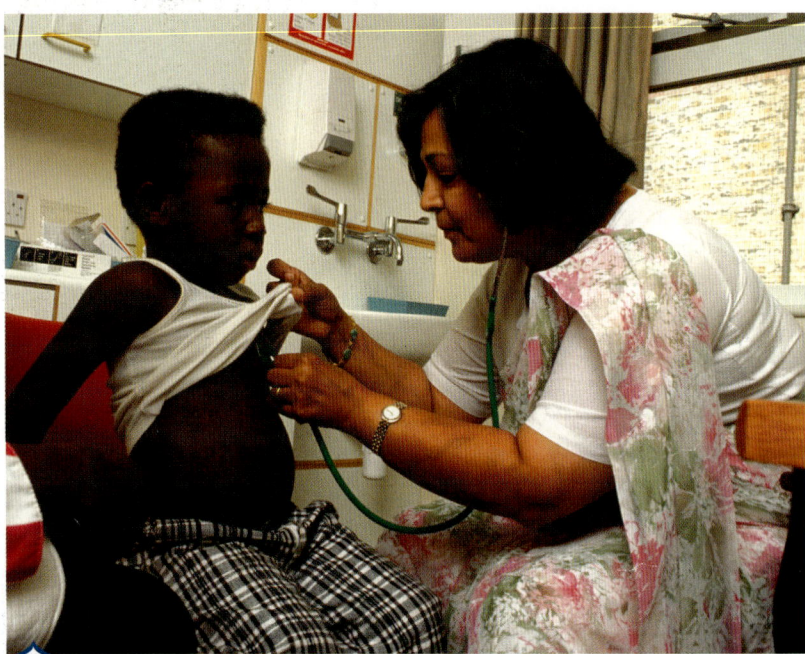

B *Working relationships*

> **Study tip**
> When asked to **name** or **identify** a relationship, you should respond with one of the following relationship types: family, friendship, intimate personal, and working. When asked to **describe** a relationship, you should add some detail: for example, Marcus works for John. The name of this relationship is a **working relationship**. To describe it, you could add that John is Marcus's **employer**.

Learning workout

Look again at the descriptions of the neighbours in the previous sections of this book. From the descriptions:
1. Name Ronan's siblings.
2. Name the two children who do not have siblings.
3. Name two children who are peers.
4. Name two people in a working relationship.
5. Name two people in an intimate sexual relationship.
6. Name the relationship between Katya and Magda.
7. Name and describe the relationship between Salma and Zena.

The effects of relationships on personal development

Relationships can have positive and negative effects on people's personal development. Remember that personal development can be categorised using PIES. The greatest effects are probably the effects of parents on their children. Here are some examples of how a relationship with parents can **positively** affect personal development in infancy and childhood:

- **Physical** Parents can provide a balanced diet for their children and provide play opportunities to help them grow and develop motor skills.
- **Intellectual** Parents can aid a child's language development by listening to them and reading books with them. Parents can provide other opportunities to learn, such as visits to museums.
- **Emotional** Parents can make sure the infant is never separated from them. This provides trust and security. Parents can set an example of acceptable ways of expressing emotions such as anger.
- **Social** Parents can set an example of acceptable ways to treat other people, such as helping, encouraging and sharing.

Here are some examples of how relationships can **negatively** affect personal development:

- **Physical** Family members can encourage each other to eat too much.
- **Intellectual** School friends can make fun of children who work hard at school.
- **Emotional** Comparing yourself with a more attractive or cleverer friend at school can reduce your self-esteem.
- **Social** Being rejected or bullied by peers at school can lead people to be unfriendly and to avoid contact with others.

C *Parents can aid a child's language development*

Study tip

Try practice question 4 at the end of this chapter (page 41).

2.4 Effects of neglect, abuse and lack of support

Within relationships, the following usually lead to negative effects on development:

- **Neglect** To neglect a person means not providing them with what they need.
- **Abuse** To abuse a person means actively harming them.
- **Lack of support** People who lack support are not helped by those who should help them.

> **Objectives**
> Define neglect, abuse and lack of support.
> Describe the effects of neglect, abuse and lack of support.

Meanwhile... in Ramsay MacDonald Street ...

Ray Webster has had a letter from Matt's school, saying that Matt has missed seven days of school in the first three weeks of term. Ray had no idea his son was not attending and asks his wife Juliet why she hasn't been making Matt go. Each of them thinks that it is the other one's responsibility to make Matt go to school.

When Matt comes home from school, Ray challenges him about his absences. Matt says he's been ill a lot, but Ray doesn't believe him. After a while, Matt starts crying and says that some other children have been bullying him. This makes Ray angry. He says, 'You mustn't cry; you're a big boy now. Don't ever let me see you crying again.'

Trying to be helpful, Ray says, 'They won't bully you if you stand up to them. You've got to give them as good as you get. They hit you; you hit them back, only harder.' He slaps Matt gently and says, 'There, I've hit you; now you hit me back.' Matt punches him weakly. Ray hits Matt harder and says, 'Hit harder.' Ray realises that he has gone too far and cuddles Matt. To comfort him, he says, 'I skipped off school a lot too. Didn't do me any harm.'

A

B Using PIES to show the effects of child neglect

Physical effects	Intellectual effects	Emotional effects	Social effects
■ Poor hygiene – not washed	■ Lack of motivation at school	■ Low self-esteem	■ Isolation
■ Body odour	■ Refusing to attend school	■ Lack of confidence	■ Poor social skills
■ Poor diet, undernourished	■ Boredom	■ Depression	■ Being bullied
■ Risk of infection or injury	■ Low achievement, e.g. poor number skills	■ Loneliness	
■ Self-harm			

Neglect

A person of any age can be neglected. The worst effects of neglect are suffered by people who are least able to look after themselves. A child who is neglected may not be given much attention, may not be washed or provided with clean or suitable clothes. A neglected child may also not be fed properly, not be treated for illnesses or injuries and not be comforted when upset. A neglected infant may be left alone for long periods and be left in a wet or dirty nappy.

C The worst effects of neglect are suffered by people who are least able to look after themselves

The effects on infants and children of these sorts of neglect can be:

- **physical** – for example, hunger, not gaining weight or growing properly, pain, frequent illness, being slow to reach motor milestones
- **intellectual** – for example, being slow to develop speech or learn concepts, having difficulty learning at school
- **emotional** – for example, unsatisfactory attachment, lack of activity or hyperactivity
- **social** – for example, being rejected by other people such as peers at school, perhaps because the child is dirty or smelly.

Abuse

Types of abuse

Bullying often includes both physical and emotional abuse. The most common form of **physical abuse** is hitting. Less common are cutting and burning.

Sexual abuse involves inappropriately touching someone's genitals or having sex with them without their consent. Sexual activity with anyone under 16 years old is also sexual abuse, even if they give their consent.

Emotional abuse involves doing things that are intended to upset, frighten or embarrass a person. One example is spreading embarrassing rumours about a person. Another is posting embarrassing photographs or text on websites. Emotional abuse is sometimes called **psychological abuse**.

Effects of abuse

One of the most common effects of abuse is on a person's emotional development. Being hit can lower a person's self-esteem. Hitting a person implies that the person is not liked or respected, and that their feelings are not important. 'I am the sort of person it is OK to hit' becomes part of that person's self-concept.

People who experience sexual abuse sometimes feel that they are partly responsible. This can lead to feelings of guilt. Emotional abuse sends the message that the person abused is disliked. All forms of abuse increase anxiety and often lead the victim to experience stress.

Lack of support

You already know how important it is for people to have support, especially when they face difficult life events. Most harmful is a lack of support from friends, partners or family members. Lack of support for children can slow down a child's intellectual development, by not encouraging learning. Generally, lack of support is bad for a person's self-esteem.

For example, there is a lack of support when:

- a parent takes no interest in a child's play or school work
- a person never gives his partner the chance to talk about things
- a child joins with other children in bullying one of her siblings
- someone notices that a friend is distressed, but ignores this.

D *Lack of support can lower self-esteem*

Study tip

Describing the effects of neglect, abuse and lack of support

It is important to use PIES when answering a question about these effects, as the question might not be about development at all. In this case, the kind of effects that are relevant might be different. Table **B** gives you an example of PIES effects on a child who is neglected.

Activity

Re-read the description of Ray and Matt (page 38). Did Ray respond to the bullying of his son in a useful way? What do you think of Ray's way of dealing with the problem? In your answer, use some of the key words in this section.

Learning workout

Use the information in Table **B** to answer the following question:

- Explain the likely negative effects on a child of being neglected by parents. *(12 marks)*

Study tip

Try practice question 5 (page 41).

Practice questions

1. Elaine is 60 years old. A lot has happened to her in the past 10 years. She has gone through the menopause, got divorced and remarried, moved house and been made redundant.

    (a) (i) Identify **two** changes in Elaine's life circumstances. *(2 marks)*

    (ii) Identify **two** changes in Elaine's relationships. *(2 marks)*

    (b) Identify **one** expected event in Elaine's life. *(1 mark)*

    (c) Describe the physical changes Elaine will have experienced during the menopause. *(3 marks)*

    (d) Describe how being made redundant might have affected Elaine's social development. *(3 marks)*

2. Carla and her husband were both aged 67 and retired. They used to go walking and swimming together several times each week. Carla's husband used to make all their holiday plans and manage their money. Now her husband has died suddenly. Evaluate the likely effects of bereavement on Carla's development. *(12 marks)*

> **Study tip**
> - Remember to think about the life stage of the person, about PIES, about whether the life event was expected or unexpected and whether the question refers to physical changes, relationship changes or changes in life circumstances.
> - Also think of positive effects as well as negative ones, and how big the effects might be.

3. Rebecca is pregnant with her first child. Her partner Simon has just lost his job and the couple often argue over money.

    Suggest **three** different sources of support to help Rebecca cope with her problems. For each source of support, give **one** different way they might help. *(6 marks)*

> **Study tip**
> - Look at the marks and the way the question is asked. You will get one mark for each source and one mark for the way the source might help.
> - Use the information from this chapter – refer to some of the listed sources of support and some of the listed ways of helping.

4 Ben has a son Alex. Alex goes to school with his friend Rahul.
Ben is employed by Lynne. Lynne has a boyfriend called Robert.

  (a) Identify the following types of relationships from the information above:
      (i) a working relationship *(1 mark)*
      (ii) a family relationship *(1 mark)*
      (iii) a peer relationship *(1 mark)*
      (iv) a friendship *(1 mark)*
      (v) an intimate personal relationship. *(1 mark)*

  (b) Describe the likely effects on Alex's development of his relationship with Ben. *(5 marks)*

> **Study tip**
>
> Remember to:
> - mention PIES
> - give one or two possible negative effects as well as positive ones
> - say something about how strong these effects might be.

5 Albert is 95 years old and suffers from neglect. He lives alone and rarely goes out. Albert finds it difficult to look after himself properly. He often goes many weeks without seeing or talking to another person. Describe the likely effects of neglect on Albert's health and wellbeing. *(10 marks)*

AQA, January 2006

> **Study tip**
>
> This is a 'problem question', because it is asking for effects on health and wellbeing, rather than development. The best advice is to use PIES, but also to make some mention of health and wellbeing in your answer.

3 Influencing factors

3.1 Factors affecting self-concept

Objectives
Identify nine factors affecting self-concept.

Explain nine effects these factors might have on self-concept.

Meanwhile...

... in Ramsay MacDonald Street ...

Zena is reading a letter that her sister Salma enclosed with her birthday card.

'Zeezee darling,

'I hope you have a nice birthday and don't get into trouble with the parents. I must tell you about Uni, it is so great. I still can't believe that I'm here. I have never met such nice people, apart from you, darling sis. It is so not like the old home town. For a start, no one is calling me a Paki. Everyone accepts everyone else. You know, when I was in school, people called me a swot and I didn't have many friends because I didn't hang out with the crowd. I used to think there was something wrong with me. Now I'm with people who think the same way as me. You can talk about anything: books, politics, films, religion, drugs, and nobody thinks you're strange. Everyone is so nice to me. It's a big effort to keep up with the work here, but I'm sure I'll manage. The lecturers are not like I thought they'd be. Most of them are young and foreign, so it's quite hard to tell what they are saying. My personal tutor's Chinese. I can't even say her name properly. I have started playing badminton again. I don't always lose, either. Nobody thinks it strange that a girl is studying chemical engineering, but most of the others are boys. That is absolutely not a problem. There are some very fit persons of the male species here – I'll tell you all about them when I'm home. Did you get the photos I emailed?

'You must promise me to keep on studying hard, and don't let the other kids get you down. Don't be like everyone else. Play it cool, like your big sis. Try to be less of an idiot and watch out for the boys. Now I'm sounding like Mama! That's all for now – I've got an essay to write.

'Love and kisses, Salma.'

Zena puts the letter down and thinks, 'If only she knew.'

A

A person's self-concept is the beliefs they have about themselves. Self-concept includes self-esteem – a person's beliefs about their own value. This is sometimes called self-worth. Self-concept also includes body-image. Body image is a person's beliefs about the size, shape and appearance of their body.

A person's self-concept is often based on the other people around them. People compare themselves with others. A child who notices that he is shorter than all his friends might think of himself as short. A child who does better in schoolwork than most of her friends might think of herself as clever.

Self-concept is also affected by what a person thinks other people think of them. The reactions of other people give the person an impression of what they are like. For example, if parents often call a child 'bad' or 'naughty', the child might think of herself as naughty. A man who gets a lot of positive attention from women might think of himself as attractive.

Notice that in these examples some of the effects on self-concept are positive, and some are negative.

> **Study tip**
> Key words are printed in blue. Remember to use these words when you are writing answers to examination questions.

Factors affecting self-concept

The following factors affect self-concept:

- life experiences, i.e. expected and unexpected events in a person's life
- age, including how mature the person is
- relationships with others, especially family and peers
- gender, i.e. the person's sex
- education, e.g. attendance at school, qualifications
- **culture**, including the person's ethnicity, beliefs, values and religion
- appearance
- sexual orientation, i.e. whether heterosexual or homosexual
- emotional development, i.e. how mature the person is in expressing and controlling emotions.

B *Culture is part of self-concept*

One way of remembering this list is to remember the words spelled out by the first letters (together they spell out the words LARGE CASE).

Effects of these factors on self-concept

These effects include making people feel:

- **successful** (or a failure)
- **proud** (or ashamed) of themselves
- a **sense of achievement** (or worthlessness)
- more (or less) **important**
- high (or low) **self-esteem**
- more (or less) **confident**
- more (or less) **comfortable** about themselves
- **optimistic** (or pessimistic) about life
- **approved of** (or disapproved of) by others.

One way of learning this list of effects is to make up a sentence with words starting with the first letters of the **emboldened** words in the list. The words in your sentence would start with S, P, S, I, S, C, C, O and A. A suitable sentence might start, 'Some people say … etc.' Of course, you could alter the order of the letters.

> **Study tip**
> Try practice question 1 at the end of this chapter (page 56).

Activity

1 This is a card game to help you learn these factors and effects. It can also help when practising answering exam questions.

a Using card of one colour make nine cards, one for each of the **LARGE CASE FACTORS**. On each card, write the name of the factor.

b Using card of a different colour, make nine cards: one for each of the emboldened **effects** listed above. On each card write the positive effect on one side and the negative effect on the other. For example, the card with **proud** on one side should have **ashamed** on the other. The card with **more comfortable** on one side should have **less comfortable** on the other.

c Pick out one **LARGE CASE FACTOR** card and then choose an **effect** card that seems to link with it.

  – For example, the cards **EDUCATION** and **sense of achievement** (or **failure**) go together well. This is because doing well at school can give a person a sense of achievement.

  – Some cards do not go well together. For example **GENDER** and **successful,** because being male or female is not something you can succeed or fail in.

  – Note that there are lots of different ways of pairing the cards.

d Once you have got all the cards paired off, try to write a sentence about each pair. The sentence should explain, or give an example of, the link. For example, if you paired **CULTURE** with **proud**, you could write, 'Megan is proud of being Welsh because she likes Welsh culture'. Another example might link **SEXUAL ORIENTATION** with **comfortable**. An example might be 'Wayne is gay and is comfortable with his sexual orientation because people accept him as he is'.

  – Try to make sure that you include some negative effects, e.g. of people feeling low self-esteem.

  – Keep these cards safe, because you will need them again for Section 3.3. They will also be useful when revising for the examination.

Activities

2 Read Salma's letter again (page 42). Pick out some of the factors affecting self-concept that she refers to and decide what effect these are having on her self-concept.

3 Read the description of Matt and Ray (page 38). Decide what effect their relationship is having on Matt's self-concept.

C *Pick out one 'factor' card and choose an 'effect' card that seems to link with it*

3.2 Factors affecting development

A person's development can be affected by the factors described in this section. Sometimes the effects are positive – they help development. Sometimes the factors are negative – they prevent or slow down development.

Differences in these factors cause **individual differences**. 'Individual differences' simply means 'differences between people'. In the examination these factors are usually called '**factors in life**', although they might sometimes be called 'factors affecting development'. The factors will be described under the headings:

- **physical factors**
- **genetic factors**
- **social and emotional factors**
- **economic factors**
- **environmental factors.**

> **Objectives**
> Describe factors affecting development.
> Give examples of each factor.
> Distinguish between needs and wants.

Physical factors

A person's growth and development is affected by their genetic make-up (sometimes called 'nature') and the influences around them (sometimes called 'nurture'). We shall now look at four physical factors affecting growth and development.

Genetic inheritance

The term '**genetic inheritance**' refers to the fact that almost everyone has a unique set of **genes**, half of which are inherited from the mother and half from the father. The unique set of genes results from an egg from the mother being fertilised by a sperm from the father at the moment of **conception**.

A gene is made up of a complex chemical called **DNA**. Most cells in the human body contain a complete set of these genes, arranged on 26 pairs of **chromosomes**. A person's genes have a big effect on growth, health, physical appearance, rate of development, personality and abilities. A person's physical appearance is strongly influenced by genes. Examples include a person's height and the colour of their skin, eyes and hair. The influence of genes on personality and abilities is less obvious.

A very small number of people have some genes that cause a disease. One example is the disease called **haemophilia**. A person with haemophilia has a deficiency in the blood so that it does not clot easily. The result is that if a person with haemophilia starts bleeding, for example from a small cut, they can lose a lot of blood. Haemophilia is very rare.

A more common condition is caused by having one extra chromosome; it is known as **Down's syndrome**. People with Down's syndrome do not usually grow as tall as other people; they have a shorter life expectancy and usually have lower than average intelligence. Another fairly common condition is **autism**; this is partly caused by genetics. People with severe autism do not develop language; they avoid contact with other people and have low intelligence.

A *The colour of a person's skin, eyes and hair is influenced by their genes*

For more information on genetically inherited diseases, see Chapter 6, The nature of health and wellbeing, pages 100–103.

Here are some examples of how genetic inheritance can affect development:

- **Physical development** A person's growth rate, height and weight are affected by their genes.
- **Intellectual development** Some children with Down's syndrome have low levels of intelligence.
- **Emotional development** Body shape is influenced by genetics and this can affect self-concept, including body image.
- **Social development** Children with autism often lack social skills and find it hard to make friends.

Diet

Diet means what a person has to eat and drink. It does not mean 'being on a diet'.

We need food for two main reasons:

- To provide us with the chemicals we need to grow and repair the body and to stay healthy.
- To provide us with chemical energy to be able to move muscles. This energy is measured in **kilocalories**. Confusingly, the term 'calorie' is sometimes used to mean the same as 'kilocalorie'.

What is a balanced diet?

A **balanced diet** is one that includes all the necessary **food components** in the right amounts. What a balanced diet is depends on the person. A balanced diet for a ballet dancer will contain more chemical energy (kilocalories) than a balanced diet for a person of the same weight who takes little exercise. A diet that includes hardly any fruit or vegetables is unlikely to be balanced for most people. It will probably lack some vitamins and minerals. But a newborn's diet will not include any fruit and vegetables. A balanced diet for a newborn will consist of milk. A person who has a balanced diet is likely to grow well and develop normally.

Too little of a food component (a **deficiency**) can be harmful. Too much of a food component (an **excess**) can also be harmful.

The necessary food components are discussed below.

Carbohydrates are important sources of food energy. Food energy means chemicals that can be used as 'fuel' to enable us to move. There are different kinds of carbohydrates, including starches and sugars. Foods rich in carbohydrates include bread, rice, pasta and sugar.

Carbohydrate can have a negative effect on health if there is too much in the diet. Then the body converts the excess food energy into fat, which can lead to the person being overweight or obese. Being overweight is a risk factor for **diabetes**, a condition in which the body cannot control the amount of sugar in the blood (for more information on diabetes, see page 48 and Chapter 6, The nature of health and wellbeing, page 106).

B *Carbohydrates provide food energy, but an excess is converted into fat*

Fibre/NSP is actually another type of carbohydrate. Fibre is not a source of energy, but it does help digestion. For example, it can prevent constipation. One type of fibre is non-starch polysaccharide, called **NSP** for short. Fibre is found in wholemeal bread, oats, peas and beans.

Fats are the most concentrated source of food energy. They occur in foods such as cooking oil, butter, margarine, bacon, cheese and nuts. The human body can make some fats from carbohydrates. The only fats we cannot make are vegetable oils. Apart from energy supply, fat also provides heat insulation, to protect the body from cold, and cushioning around delicate organs, such as the eyes.

A negative effect on health occurs if there is too much fat in the diet. Excess fat is stored around the body and leads to overweight or **obesity** (being very overweight; see page 48).

Cholesterols are fats which circulate in the blood. Eating meat products that are high in fat, such as bacon and sausages, and dairy products, such as butter, tends to increase cholesterol levels. A diet with more oily fish and less meat and dairy products lowers harmful cholesterol. The main problem with cholesterol in the blood is that it can stick to the inside of blood vessels, making them narrower and leading to heart disease, which prevents the heart from working properly (for more on heart disease, see page 49 and Chapter 6, The nature of health and wellbeing, page 84).

Proteins are needed for growth, because they help to build up muscle. They are also used in the repair and maintenance of body tissues. Proteins occur in foods that are the muscles of other animals, such as meat and fish. Proteins are also found in nuts, eggs, milk, cheese, peas and beans.

Minerals are chemical elements that are needed for building body tissues. They do not contain food energy. They include iron, calcium, and phosphorus. Iron is found in meat and is an important component of blood. Calcium is found in milk and cheese and is important in the growth of bones and teeth. Phosphorus is also important in the growth of bones and teeth. It is found in many foods, especially vegetables.

Excessive intake of some minerals is harmful. For example, eating too much common salt can increase blood pressure. A deficiency of minerals can cause illness. For example, a lack of iron can cause a shortage of red blood cells, called **anaemia**. A lack of calcium can restrict the growth of bones and teeth in children.

Vitamins are important ingredients in the chemical reactions that enable body cells to function and grow. They contain very little food energy. Different vitamins are found in fruit (e.g. vitamin C) and oily fish (e.g. vitamin D). Vitamins A is found in liver, eggs, milk and carrots. It helps the growth and repair of cells in the skin and eyes.

An excess of some vitamins (caused by taking vitamin supplement pills) can be harmful to health. A deficiency of vitamins can cause illness. For example, a lack of vitamin D can restrict the growth of bones and teeth in children.

> **Study tip**
> Make a list of the main food components i.e. carbohydrates, fibre, fats, etc and for each one write down three foods that contain this component. Then learn your list.

C *Fruit and vegetables are a good source of vitamins*

Water

Water is the basis for many liquids found inside the body, such as the blood and the liquid that lubricates joints. Water is present in drinks, fruit and vegetables.

Macronutrients and micronutrients

Carbohydrates, fats and proteins are called macronutrients. Minerals and vitamins are micronutrients because they are only required in small amounts.

Dietary problems

A **poor-quality diet** is a diet which is deficient (or lacks) one or more of the food components. An example is a deficiency in vitamin C, which used to cause long-distance sailors to suffer from the disease scurvy. Vitamin C is found in fruit, especially oranges. It helps wounds to heal.

Over-consumption of foods can lead to a build-up of fat in the body. A person who eats more energy foods (fats and carbohydrates) than the body needs is likely to become obese. An excess of fats in the diet can lead to high levels of cholesterol in the blood.

Having a diet which involves over-consumption or deficiency is called malnutrition. Here are some examples of how diet can affect development:

- **Physical** A good diet enables growth. A poor diet can lead to disease (e.g. obesity, high blood pressure, diabetes and heart disease). Sugary foods and drinks can lead to tooth decay.
- **Intellectual** Under-nourishment can slow intellectual development.
- **Emotional** Obesity can lead to a negative body image and low self-esteem.
- **Social** Poor diet can reduce social contact if it leads to obesity.

Disease

Diseases include infections caused by **bacteria** and **viruses**, (e.g. the flu virus); damage to body tissues, caused by toxic chemicals such as alcohol and tobacco smoke; dietary deficiencies or excess; and genetic disorders. Some common diseases are discussed below.

Obesity

Obesity is a common condition in which a person's body has a very large amount of stored fat. There are several causes, including a diet with too much carbohydrate and fat and taking too little exercise. Obesity can cause high blood pressure, diabetes, heart disease and loss of mobility. It also increases the risk of getting cancer. It can be treated by reducing food intake and increasing exercise.

Diabetes

Diabetes is an illness in which the body cannot control the amount of sugar in the blood. It is incurable, but the effects can be controlled using drugs. If not treated in this way, diabetes can lead to other diseases including high blood pressure, strokes and heart disease.

Activities

1. Write down what you have eaten and drunk in the last 24 hours.
2. Decide which the main food components are in each item that you consumed.
3. Now decide whether your diet during those 24 hours was balanced.

links

For more information on the effects of diet, see the summary table in Chapter 6, page 91.

Study tip

Try practice question 2 at the end of this chapter (page 56).

D *Obesity can cause high blood pressure, diabetes and heart disease*

Heart disease

The heart pumps blood around the body. Heart disease includes a range of illnesses which mean that the heart does not work as well as the body requires. This results in a person feeling weak and very short of breath.

Cancer

Cancer is an illness in which some body cells start multiplying uncontrollably. This causes two problems. One is that the cells build up into a large mass called a tumour, which can press on other body tissues and stop them working. Another problem is that the tumour uses the body's own blood supply and so deprives other body tissues. Some cancers can spread to different parts of the body.

Here are some examples of how disease can affect development:

- **Physical** Disease can restrict children's growth and reduce strength and mobility in older people.
- **Intellectual** Pain can make it difficult to concentrate.
- **Emotional** Diseases that reduce mobility can leave people feeling depressed.
- **Social** Disease can lead to social isolation if a person is not mobile.

Physical activity

Physical activity is important for development in infancy, childhood and adolescence because it helps in building muscles. Physical activity also helps weight control, because it uses up food energy which might otherwise be stored as excess fat.

Most infants and children are normally very active. If activity is prevented, for example by disease, bone and muscle growth can be less than normal. Physical activity includes exercise. Adolescents and adults are normally less active and so have to take exercise to remain healthy. Exercise helps to maintain stamina, speed, strength and flexibility.

Here are some examples of how physical activity can affect development:

- **Physical** Exercise can increase strength, speed, stamina, mobility and flexibility. It can also help control a person's weight, which makes them less likely to develop diseases.
- **Intellectual** It can be easier to concentrate after physical activity.
- **Emotional** Exercise often makes people feel more contented and helps to combat depression.
- **Social** Physical activities bring people together, enabling friendships to be made.

E *Physical activity can increase strength, speed, stamina, mobility and flexibility, as well as helping with weight control*

Activity

4 Work out how much physical activity you have had in the past week.
   a List the physical activities you have taken part in for each day.
   b Now work out roughly how long each activity took. For example, if you walk to school or college, add up the time taken doing this in a week.
   c Now work out the average amount of time you spend in physical activity each day and compare this with the time spent by your peers.

Study tip

Try practice question 3 at the end of this chapter (page 56).

Genetic factors

Exam questions sometimes ask for 'genetic factors'. In an exam question, this means those features of a person that are partly or mainly influenced by a person's genes. Examples of these factors are skin colour, hair colour, eye colour and height.

Social and emotional factors

Development can be affected by social and emotional factors. These include:

- gender (the sex of a person)
- family relationships including experiences of divorce, support, neglect or abuse
- friendships
- educational experiences, including qualifications gained
- employment or unemployment
- **ethnicity** and religion – ethnicity means a person's race, nationality, culture and religion
- life experiences including birth, marriage, divorce and death.

This list is quite similar to the list of factors affecting self-concept described at the beginning of this chapter (page 43).

Here are some examples of how social and emotional factors can affect development:

- **Physical** The gender (sex) of a person affects growth around puberty.
- **Intellectual** Education affects a person's development of language and thinking skills.
- **Emotional** Being unemployed can increase the risk of depression.
- **Social** Getting married and having children causes big changes to a person's social circle.

Economic factors

Economic factors affecting development include:

- a person's **income**, for example their wages, salary or cash benefits received
- a person's **material possessions** – the things they own.

A family's income might have an effect on the development of an infant or child. A high level of income should enable the child to develop to their potential. For example, it will enable the family to afford a balanced diet, buy equipment used in sport and **leisure**, and pay for tuition in music and dance, etc. Compared with the majority of the world's population, people in Britain have a high level of income. (For more on financial resources and on leisure, see Chapter 6, The nature of health and wellbeing, pages 114 and 117.)

A person's material possessions can affect their development. For example, if a person owns a car they might get less exercise than a person who walks or cycles to work. Families are sometimes not able to afford to provide children with all they require for normal development. This can happen if money is spent on **wants** (things people like to have) rather than on **needs** (essentials).

F *This child's family can afford music lessons*

Here are some examples of how economic factors can affect development:

- **Physical** A person who can afford gym membership might get plenty of exercise.
- **Intellectual** Children whose parents own many books have more opportunities to learn.
- **Emotional** Having plenty of money can make people feel secure, and prevent money worries.
- **Social** People with plenty of money can afford to visit relatives abroad.

Needs and wants

Needs are things that it is essential for people to have. These include water, food (a balanced diet) and protection from the environment (clothes and shelter). Other possible essentials are some form of energy supply, such as gas or electricity, and materials used to maintain hygiene, such as soap. Some people would add money to this list, although we only need it to buy the other things.

Wants are things that people like to have, but which are not essential for survival or normal development. Examples include mobile phones, fashionable shoes, televisions, cars and jewellery.

Environmental factors

Environmental factors affecting development include:

- **housing conditions** – e.g. availability of space, overcrowding, ease of cleaning, presence of damp, presence of vermin, heating, risk of falls
- **the surrounding area** – e.g. whether in a town or the country, whether there is good transport, levels of crime, etc.
- **pollution** – e.g. noise from vehicles or neighbours, air pollution from vehicle smoke, litter
- **access to** (health and welfare) **services** – e.g. whether the client has to pay, how easy it is to get to the service, whether there is a waiting list.

Housing conditions

Housing conditions can affect growth and development in several ways:

- **Physical** Lack of heating can lead to **hypothermia** (a potentially fatal condition that occurs when the core body temperature falls below 35 °C. Dampness can cause mould to grow and this can make allergies and respiratory illnesses worse. Housing that is dirty, lacks hot water or is difficult to clean can increase the risk of infections.
- **Intellectual** Plenty of living space gives children more opportunities to play. Children, adolescents and adults can also work or study undisturbed.
- **Emotional** Overcrowded housing can increase conflict within a family and increase the risk of stress.
- **Social** High levels of crime in the neighbourhood can make people afraid to go out, and they may lose social contact.

G *Plenty of living space enables family members to study undisturbed*

Surrounding area and pollution

These can also affect development:

- **Physical** Availability of parks in the surrounding area can provide exercise opportunities. Air pollution, such as vehicle smoke, can increase respiratory infections.
- **Intellectual** Noise pollution at night can lead to lack of sleep, causing tiredness and poor concentration.
- **Emotional** Noisy neighbours can cause stress.
- **Social** A built-up area usually means that there are many opportunities to meet people, for example at youth clubs.

Access to health and welfare services

Access to health and welfare services refers to several factors:

- **Whether or not a particular service is available** In some parts of Britain, it is easier to get access to a service such as education for children with special educational needs. In some places, GPs are able to prescribe some expensive drugs, but in other parts there is not enough money to do this. This is sometimes called a '**postcode lottery**'.
- **How easy or difficult it is to get to the service** In towns it is usually easier to get to services than it is in the country. This is because the size of the population means that there are plenty of GP surgeries, day centres, etc. Usually, there is also better public transport in towns.
- **How easy or difficult it is to get into the service** Some people have difficulty in getting an appointment with a GP because they work during the day and the surgery is not open in the evening. In some areas, there are not enough places in residential homes for all the older people who need them.

> **Study tip**
> When you write Assignment 1 for this Unit you will have to say how services are structured. If one of services you describe is integrated, you must say this very clearly. You might write, 'In this area local authority Social Services work together with the NHS to provide this service.'

> **Study tip**
> Try practice questions 4 and 5 at the end of this chapter (page 56–57).

Activity

5 This activity also involves making cards. Use card of a different colour from the cards you used for the factors affecting self-concept.

a Cut out 17 cards and write the following words on each one:

genetic inheritance   housing conditions
friendships   income   employment
ethnicity   pollution   family relationships
educational experiences   life experiences
diet   surrounding area   access to services
physical activity   gender   disease
material possessions

b Label each card 'Factors in life'. On the back of each card, write a few words giving details. For example, on the back of the card marked 'diet' you might write 'balanced', and 'food components'. On the back of the card marked 'pollution' you might write 'noise', 'smoke', 'litter'. Now use the cards to learn this information. There are several ways to do this.

– **The flip side game**

Pick a card (either way up) and try to remember what is written on the other side. For example, if you picked up the card saying 'noise, smoke, litter', you might remember that on the other side is the word 'pollution'. If you picked up the card saying 'diet', you might remember that the words 'balanced' and 'food components' were on the other side. You could play this as a game with another student, taking turns to take a card and keeping it if you get it right. When all the cards have been used, the winning player is the one with most cards.

– **The sorting game**

Another way to use these cards is to sort them into groups using the following headings: 'physical factors', 'social and emotional factors', 'economic factors' and 'environmental factors'.

– **Revision**

When revising for the exam, keep testing yourself with these cards.

3.3 Effects of factors in a person's life

The effects of the factors in life on a person's development have already been described. In this section, we look at the effects of these 17 factors on:

- self-esteem
- health and wellbeing – i.e. physical and mental health
- employment prospects – i.e. the person's chances of getting a job and the sort of job
- level of education – i.e. how much education they have had and how well they did.

> **Objectives**
>
> State the effects of factors in life on self-esteem, health and wellbeing, employment prospects, level of education and development.

Effects of factors in life on self-esteem

Activity

1 Use the 'Factors in life' cards you made for Activity 5 on page 52. For each factor, try to think of an example of how that factor affects a person's self-esteem. You will find this easier if you use your set of nine '**effects**' cards that you made for the Activity on page 44.

a Pick one of the 'Factors in life' cards, and one of the '**effects**' cards, at random.
  – For example, you might pick out 'housing conditions' and '**ashamed**'.
  – Then make up a sentence linking the two cards: for example, 'Gail feels ashamed because her house is damp and dirty'.

b Try this for each of the factors in life, and then compare your sentences with what other students have written.

Effects of factors in life on health and wellbeing

Health and wellbeing includes:

- physical health – i.e. a person's fitness and whether or not the person has any illnesses
- mental health – e.g. whether or not the person is anxious or depressed
- general wellbeing – i.e. a person's level of happiness and satisfaction with life.

Activity

2 Once again use the 17 'Factors in life' cards and for each factor try to think of an example of how that factor affects a person's health and wellbeing. You might be able to link some of the factors to diseases mentioned on page 48, such as diabetes or heart disease.

Some links are easier than others to think of. Some of the less obvious links are given in the following examples; the factor in life is shown in bold:

a Jonah's **ethnicity** makes it more likely that he will have a type of anaemia.

b Having a **disease** causes Layla to be often depressed.

c **Life experiences** such as being sexually abused can increase the risk of mental illness.

d **Gender** can affect disease, because only males have haemophilia.

Effects of factors in life on employment prospects

Some factors in life do not directly affect a person's employment prospects at all, but others do. For example **gender** and **ethnicity** might affect employment prospects if an employer discriminated in favour of or against a particular sex or nationality. A man might find it difficult to get employment as a nanny, and a woman might find it easier to get a job as an engineer in a company that discriminated in favour of women. Some of the less obvious links are given in the following examples:

- **Employment** might affect a person's employment prospects, because their existing experience of work might make them more suitable.
- **Material possessions** might affect a person's employment prospects. For example, a job might require a person to have their own car.
- **Housing conditions** might affect a person's employment. For example, if the job involved working from home, the home has to be big enough to allow this.

Effects of factors in life on level of education

As with employment, some of these factors do not directly affect a person's level of education at all.

A *A job might require a person to have their own car*

> **Activity**
>
> 3 Remember the 17 factors in life (use the cards from the Activity if you need to). For each factor, try to think of an example of how that factor affects a person's employment prospects.

> **Learning workout**
>
> Answering the following questions will help you see some of the more obvious links. The factor in life is shown in bold.
>
> 1 How might **disease** have a direct effect on how much education a child receives?
> 2 Think of one **material possession** that would help an adolescent with their education.
> 3 Adolescents tend to be influenced by their peers. Think of one way your **friends** are influencing your level of education.
> 4 Think of one **educational experience** you have had that has influenced your attitude to education, and therefore your level of education.
> 5 **Housing conditions** How might not having a room to yourself at home affect your level of education?
> 6 **Family relationships** Think of one thing a parent could do that would increase a child's level of education.

> **Activity**
>
> 4 Once again, think about the 17 factors in life. For each factor try to think of an example of how that factor affects a person's level of education. Do not worry if you cannot find examples in every case.

> **Study tip**
>
> Try practice question 6 at the end of this chapter (page 57).

3.4 How factors inter-relate

This section uses the information you have learned so far to answer a question about how factors in life interrelate to affect a person's:

- self-esteem
- health and wellbeing
- employment prospects
- level of education
- personal development.

What does 'inter-relate' mean?

'Inter-relate' means that some of the 17 factors of life are connected with each other and combine to cause effects on self-esteem and so on. There are three ways in which factors in life might do this:

- One factor might cause another factor, which then has an effect.
  - For example, air pollution might cause a disease that could limit a person's ability to work (employment prospects).
- Two (or more) factors might both have a similar effect.
  - For example, a poor diet and lack of physical activity might cause a person to develop a disease (e.g. obesity).
- Two (or more) factors might have opposite effects (e.g. one positive and one negative).

So, to answer an 'inter-relate' question, you should show how some of the factors can be linked together and how they can affect self-esteem, health and wellbeing, employment prospects, level of education or personal development.

For example, if asked about the interrelation of factors that affect level of education, you could explain that a family's **income** affects what sort of **home** they can afford, as well as what **material possessions** they have. You could say that having a large income enables the family to buy a computer to help a child study, and having a large home means that there will probably be a room where the child can study without being interrupted or distracted by other family members.

> **Objectives**
>
> Explain how factors in life inter-relate.

> **Activities**
>
> 1. Use your 'Factors in life' cards. Pick out two or three factors that might have a combined effect on self-esteem. Write a sentence linking the factors and self-esteem.
> 2. Now try the same with factors affecting:
>   a. health and wellbeing
>   b. employment prospects
>   c. education
>   d. personal development.
>
> Note that personal development is about PIES.

> **Study tip**
>
> When you write Assignment 1 for this Unit you will have to say how the services you describe are accessed. Remember to use the words 'self-referral', 'professional referral' and 'third-party referral'.

> **Study tip**
>
> **Answering 'inter-relate' questions**
>
> - Refer to what is said in the description.
> - Use the appropriate names of factors in life.
> - Describe how two or more of these factors are linked.
> - Explain how they cause effects – give reasons.
> - Use key terms, e.g. names of diseases.
> - Refer to PIES if the question is about development.
> - Say whether the effects are positive or negative – and give both.
> - Suggest how great the effects might be – don't overstate them.

> **Study tip**
>
> Try practice question 7 (on page 57).

Practice questions

1 Mark is 40 years old and nearly bald. His job has enabled him to travel all over the world. He was recently divorced and now lives alone. Because he is good at managing difficult situations, he has just been promoted at work.

Identify **four** different factors which may affect Mark's self-concept.
For each factor explain how it may have an effect. *(12 marks)*

> **Study tip**
> The word 'Identify' means that examples of the factors are included in the description. Six of the factors are included, and you only need four. First try to pick out the six factors, and then decide which four will give you the best answers. Make sure that you link each factor you identify with one of the LARGE CASE factors, such as life experience.

2 (a) Explain how genetic inheritance can affect a person's physical and intellectual development. *(6 marks)*
   (b) Explain how diet can affect a person's emotional and social development. *(6 marks)*

3 (a) Maureen has bought a trampoline for her children to use in the garden. Explain how using the trampoline might affect her children's motor development. *(4 marks)*
   (b) Maureen does not want to use the trampoline herself, because she is overweight. Suggest another physical activity that Maureen could do. Explain how this could affect Maureen's physical development. *(8 marks)*

4 Lena is a girl with brown hair and brown eyes. She has been ill in a hospital near her home for several weeks and has missed time at school. While she was in hospital her friends and parents visited her.
From the description above, identify:
   (a) **one** physical factor *(1 mark)*
   (b) **one** environmental factor *(1 mark)*
   (c) **two** genetic factors *(2 marks)*
   (d) **three** social and emotional factors. *(3 marks)*

5 (a) Suggest **three** environmental factors and outline **one** negative effect each one might have on a person's development. *(9 marks)*

(b) Give **two** physical factors and explain how these might affect the development of an adolescent. *(10 marks)*

6 Gordon lives rough, mostly sleeping in a city centre park. He carries everything he owns in a plastic bag. He has lost contact with his family, after a long period of mental illness. He is sent for a job interview by a job centre.

(a) From the description above, identify:
  (i) **one** physical factor *(1 mark)*
  (ii) **one** social factor *(1 mark)*
  (iii) **one** economic factor *(1 mark)*
  (iv) **one** environmental factor. *(1 mark)*

(b) Explain how the factors in Gordon's life might affect his employment prospects. *(8 marks)*

7 (a) Dewi lives in a large house in a good neighbourhood. He spends a lot of time at work and does not have much time for family activities. Dewi earns a good salary and likes taking holidays abroad and having a new car every three years. He does not have many friends.

Identify the following factors in Dewi's life:
  (i) **one** environmental factor *(1 mark)*
  (ii) **two** economic factors *(2 marks)*
  (iii) **two** social factors. *(2 marks)*

(b) Explain how the different factors in Dewi's life may inter-relate to affect his self-esteem. *(9 marks)*

AQA, January 2005

4 Needs and services

4.1 Introduction to Unit 2

For this unit you have to produce two separate written assignments. The two assignments should be submitted in one file. The first assignment is about the health and wellbeing needs of one client, and how those needs are met. Your client will fit into one of the following client groups:

- infancy (0–3 years)
- childhood (4–10 years)
- adolescence (11–18 years)
- adulthood (19–65 years)
- later adulthood (65+ years)
- disabled people.

This chapter contains basic information for Assignment 1.

The second assignment is about the job roles and skills of any three care workers. Basic information for Assignment 2 will be found in Chapter 5, Job roles and skills.

> **Objectives**
> Identify the needs of clients.
> Describe care sectors and organisation.

■ The needs of clients

For Assessment 1, you have to identify the needs of a client. What are these needs? Once again, the client's needs can mostly be described using PIES:

- **Physical needs** include illness prevention, treatment for illness (such as medication), hygiene, food (diet), sleep, exercise, mobility, accommodation (warmth and shelter) and safety.
- **Intellectual needs** include information about the client's health condition, and about treatment, stimulation and learning opportunities.
- **Emotional needs** include attention, affection, approval, security, self-esteem, and emotional stability.
- **Social needs** include social contact and interaction with other people and opportunities to develop and use social skills.

A *Children need space to play*

The following types of need overlap with those above:

- **health needs** (e.g. illness prevention and treatment, diet, exercise and hygiene)
- **developmental needs**
  - **physical** (e.g. diet, exercise, play space)
  - **intellectual** (e.g. play materials; contact with competent carers, such as parents; experience of language)
  - **emotional** (e.g. reliable presence of adult for attachment)
  - **social** (e.g. play opportunities with peers and adults)
  - **educational needs** (e.g. opportunities to learn skills, including communication skills; and life skills, such as parenting and self-care; healthy lifestyle).

How services are organised

Service type and care sector

The services you should know about divide into three types:

- **Health care services** These include **primary health care**, which means services available in the community, especially GPs; and **secondary health care**, which means services provided in hospital.
- **Social or community care services** These are sometimes organised into services for adults and services for children.
- **Early years services** These are mainly for childcare and education.

The sectors involved in providing these services also divide into three types:

- the statutory sector
- the private sector
- the voluntary sector.

B Hospitals provide health care services

The statutory sector

Services in the statutory sector are typically provided free to everyone who has a need for them. The main organisations in this sector are the National Health Service (NHS) and the Social Services departments of local authorities (i.e. city, county or borough councils). Statutory services are paid for out of various kinds of taxation. The other sectors, described below, are sometimes called the 'non-statutory' sector.

The private sector

This means organisations or individuals who provide services so as to make a profit. These services have to be paid for. Some private sector services are alternatives to statutory services. For example, a person can buy an operation in a private hospital. Some private sector services are not alternatives to statutory services but make up for a lack of statutory provision. For example, there are not enough NHS dentists to provide treatment for everyone who needs it, and private dental clinics make up the difference.

The voluntary sector

Unlike the private sector, voluntary sector organisations do not make a profit. Most of them aim to provide services free or at very low cost. Some people who work for these organisations are full time and paid, for example people who work for the National Society for the Prevention of Cruelty to Children (NSPCC). Some are unpaid volunteers, for example telephone listeners for Samaritans.

Voluntary sector services are paid for by a combination of charity contributions, grants from local or national government and payments from clients.

C *Charities often use unpaid volunteers to deliver their services*

D *Examples of services in different sectors*

Sector	Health care	Social/community care	Early years
Statutory	NHS hospital care	Local authority social services	Local authority nursery schools
Private	Optician	Private residential care home	Childminders
Voluntary	The Family Planning Association	Charity care homes	Pre-School Playgroups Association

The structure of services

The structure of the NHS is shown in Source **E**. Note that this is a simplified structure. A number of other organisations are involved, including Foundation Trusts in some areas and Special Health Authorities.

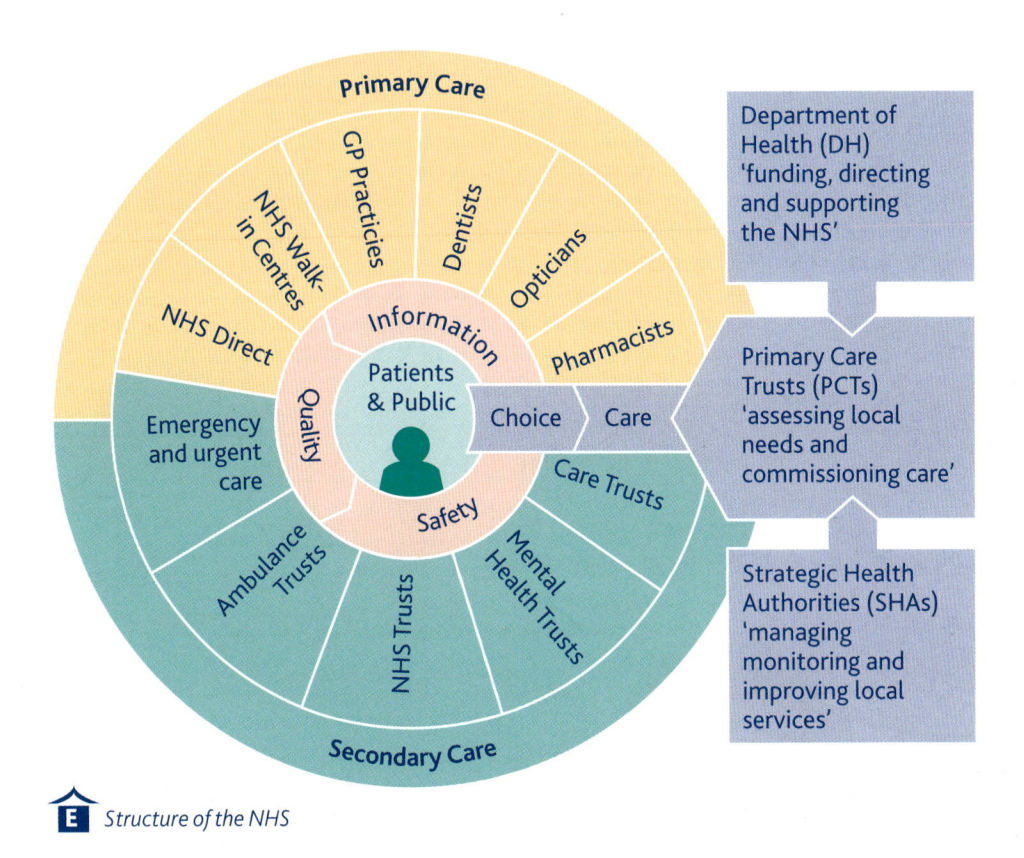

Primary Care: GP Practices, Dentists, Opticians, Pharmacists, NHS Walk-in Centres, NHS Direct

Secondary Care: Emergency and urgent care, Ambulance Trusts, NHS Trusts, Mental Health Trusts, Care Trusts

Centre: Patients & Public — Information, Choice, Care, Safety, Quality

- Department of Health (DH) 'funding, directing and supporting the NHS'
- Primary Care Trusts (PCTs) 'assessing local needs and commissioning care'
- Strategic Health Authorities (SHAs) 'managing monitoring and improving local services'

E *Structure of the NHS*

Integrated services

Until recently, community health services (i.e. primary health care services) were run by the NHS and social services were run by local authorities (e.g. county or borough councils). One problem with this system is that different organisations working with the same client did not always communicate well with each other.

Now in many areas community health and social care services are combined. This has the advantage that the two services communicate with each other better. This is sometimes called **partnership working**. The same person might be Chief Executive of a primary care trust (PCT) and Director of Social Services. This means that structure diagrams can get quite complicated.

In some areas, the organisations overseeing these **integrated services** are called care trusts.

> **Study tip**
>
> When you write Assignment 1 for this Unit you will have to say how services are structured. If one of the services you describe is integrated, you must say this very clearly. You might write, 'In this area local authority Social Services work together with the NHS to provide this service.'

4.2 Access to services and barriers to access

How people get access to services

People get access to services through referral; there are three different types:

- **Self-referral** means that a person can access a service by asking for it themselves. One example is making an appointment with a GP. Another is by going to an Accident and Emergency department.
- A **professional referral** means that a professional care worker arranges a service for you. You cannot arrange it directly yourself. An example is having an ultrasound scan. You cannot ask for one yourself, but your GP can request one for you. A GP, social worker or other professional will only make a professional referral if they judge that you need it.
- In a **third-party referral**, another person who is not a health or social care professional arranges the service for you. One example is a neighbour telephoning to arrange for someone to have a flu vaccination. Another example is a teacher contacting a social worker about a child who is at risk of abuse. Referrals for infants and children are usually made by their parents. These are also third-party referrals.

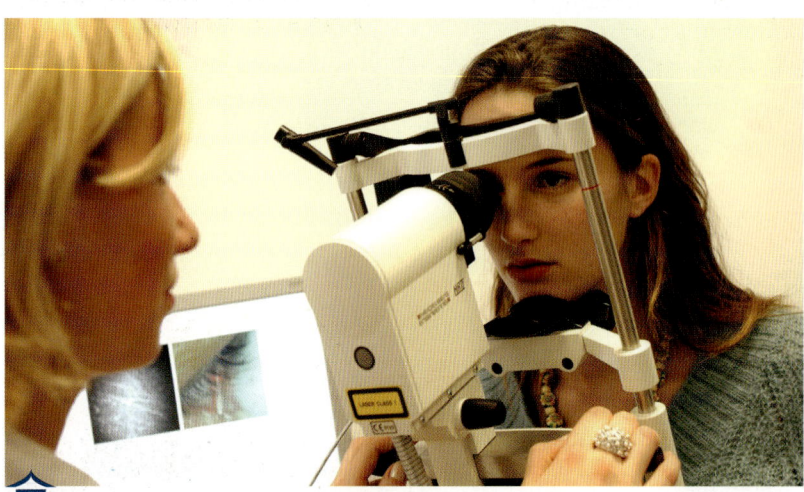

A People get access to services through referral

Barriers to access

A barrier to access is anything that makes it difficult for a person to receive a service that they need.

Barriers can be:

- physical
- psychological
- financial
- geographical
- cultural, including language
- lack of resources.

Objectives
Describe methods of referral.
Describe barriers to access.

Study tip
If you are a client receiving a health or social care service, look out for staff using some of these skills. For example after you have been to the dentist note down which of these skills they used.

Activity
1. For each example below, identify which of the three methods of referral is being used.
   a. A son arranges for his mother to have an appointment with an optician.
   b. A health visitor arranges for an infant to be seen by a paediatrician (a doctor who specialises in child health).
   c. A man who has broken his arm takes a taxi to the Accident and Emergency department of a hospital.

Physical barriers

A **physical barrier** to access means that a client cannot get into a building or part of a building in which the service is provided. This might affect a client with a **mobility problem**, for example someone who could not climb stairs or who uses a wheelchair. In this case, the barriers might be that there are stairs but no lifts, doors that are hard for a wheelchair user to open, and no disabled toilet.

Psychological barriers

A **psychological barrier** is one caused by a client's beliefs, fears or ignorance. A client might not visit the GP because they are afraid to find out that they have a serious illness. A client might not want to move into a residential home, because they fear that they will lose their independence. A client might not know about a service.

Financial barriers

A **financial barrier** occurs when a client cannot afford to pay for a service. This applies mainly to private services, such as private dental treatment. NHS services are mainly free, apart from prescription charges in England and even these are free for poorer people.

Geographical barriers

A **geographical barrier** means having difficulty in travelling to a service. This might be because the client lives in a rural area, a long way from the service, does not have a car, and there is not much local public transport.

B *This wheelchair user is experiencing a physical barrier to access*

Cultural and language barriers

A **cultural barrier** occurs when a person's culture makes it hard for them to accept a service. For example, people from one culture might not like male care workers to give treatment or personal care to female clients. A **language barrier** happens when a care worker and a client do not speak the same language, so that they cannot understand each other.

Resource barriers

Resources are needed to run services. Resources include money, staff, buildings and equipment. For example, a residential home might not be able to get enough care assistants. There might not be enough funding to keep a hospital department open. There might be more demand for a service than the organisation can supply.

Resource barriers might affect clients in two ways. One way is that clients might not be able to receive the service at all. Another is that clients might have to wait a long time to get the service.

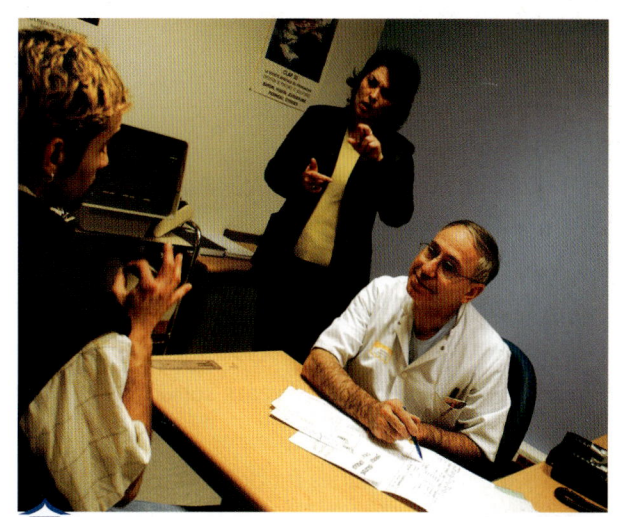

C *Sign interpreters may be needed for a care worker and a deaf client*

4.3 Services – needs, aims and care actions

The aim of this section is to introduce you to what services and care workers actually do to meet clients' needs. You will find this section useful when writing Assignment 1. Three care services are described as examples. You will have to do your own research on other care services that clients might use, but these examples will help you to know what to look for.

Different services have different sets of aims, although these often overlap. These aims are mainly to do with fulfilling the needs of clients.

> **Objectives**
> Describe service aims.
> Explain how care actions meet client needs.

■ Service aims

Here are some examples of service aims applying to different clients or services.

Typical service aims in **health care** include:

- diagnosing illness
- treating illness
- aiding recovery and rehabilitation
- preventing illness
- monitoring health and wellbeing
- providing information about illness and treatment.

Typical service aims in **social care** (such as in residential homes) include:

- providing a balanced diet
- providing a safe living environment
- providing opportunities for sleep and rest
- providing personal hygiene
- providing personal care
- providing emotional security
- providing warmth and shelter
- providing stimulation
- providing opportunities for physical activity
- empowering clients, promoting independence
- providing clients with attention, approval and security
- protecting clients from abuse and neglect
- providing social contact.

Typical service aims in **early years services** include:

- providing learning opportunities
- providing opportunities for development.

Typical service aims for people with **disabilities** include:

- providing advice, guidance and information
- supplying aids for mobility
- supplying aids for hearing and vision
- advising on adaptations to aid daily living.

A *One service aim is to aid recovery and rehabilitation*

Care actions – how needs are met

Care actions are the particular things that care workers do to meet the needs of clients. For example, GP services aim to diagnose illnesses, to treat minor illnesses and to refer patients to hospital for more specialist treatment. A GP also aims to provide information to patients about their condition and treatment.

The care actions involved in providing GP services include:

- asking a patient questions about symptoms and about other relevant factors such as the patient's job, lifestyle and physical activity
- observing the patient's appearance and using monitoring equipment (e.g. to measure blood pressure)
- testing for signs of disease (e.g. by feeling parts of the patient's body, using a stethoscope to listen to the patient's breathing); asking a practice nurse to take a blood sample for testing at a pathology laboratory
- diagnosing illness, i.e. deciding what is probably wrong with the patient
- providing treatments (e.g. lancing an abscess; giving an injection; writing a prescription for medical drugs); treatment can include minor surgery
- referring the patient to other services (e.g. to a hospital specialist, a community nurse, an occupational therapist)
- explaining to the patient what is wrong with them and what effects the treatment might have
- providing reassurance to overanxious patients
- advising patients about how to improve their own health (e.g. by giving up smoking)
- updating patients' medical records
- working with other members of the GP surgery or health centre team in order to arrange future appointments, arrange tests for **screening**.

B *One of many care actions – using a stethoscope to listen to a patient's breathing*

Services for different client groups

Note that services for disabled people differ according to the type of **impairment** the person has. Impairments are sometimes divided up into three types:

- **Physical impairments** These are problems with motor behaviour. Examples include the inability to walk because of the loss of a leg or because of arthritis or motor neurone disease.
- **Sensory impairments** This term mainly refers to deafness, partial hearing, blindness or partial sight.
- **Learning impairments** This term mainly refers to low intelligence, due either to brain damage or disease.

4.4 Researching Assignment 1

■ Choosing a client

Assignment 1 requires you to write about the needs of just one client and describe the services that meet the client's needs. You should choose a client carefully. A good choice is a person who has a number of health and social problems. You might have an older relative who would not mind being studied.

Another good choice is a person who has a disability that gives rise to several health and social problems. In any case, you should make sure that the client you choose is receiving **two** of the following:

- health care services
- social care services
- early years services.

Other reasonable choices are a pregnant woman or an infant.

You should ask the person's permission to use them as the client for this assignment. In the case of infants and children, you should ask the parent's permission too.

■ Researching needs and access

You should find out about your client's needs. Don't ask, 'What are your physical needs, intellectual needs, etc.' Instead you should ask about any illnesses they have, what treatment they are getting, and what other problems they have. In the case of an infant, you should ask the parent about any health conditions, vaccinations, attendance at a crèche, etc. Make notes of this information.

If you already know the client well, you will know about some of these illnesses, problems or needs. Some will be obvious. For example, you will be able to observe whether or not the client wears glasses, has a hearing aid, uses a wheelchair or lives on their own.

Needs means 'PIES', so remember to ask questions that will give you information not just about physical needs but also about intellectual, emotional and social needs. It's up to you to remember what these needs are and ask questions that the client will understand. For example, you might remember that intellectual needs include stimulation and information, so you might ask, 'Did the doctor explain why she was giving you the injection?' or 'What sort of things do you do at the day centre?'

You should also try to find out how easy it has been for the client to get access to their treatment. For example, how did they get to their hospital appointments, or have they waited a long time to get an appointment? Make notes of this information.

■ Researching services

When you ask your client about services that the client has used or is using, remember to ask what the care worker actually did. For example, ask what the physiotherapist did. The client might say that the physiotherapist asked questions, stretched and manipulated the client's leg, suggested exercises to do, etc.

Objectives
Plan and research needs, access and services.

A A pregnant woman is a possible choice of client

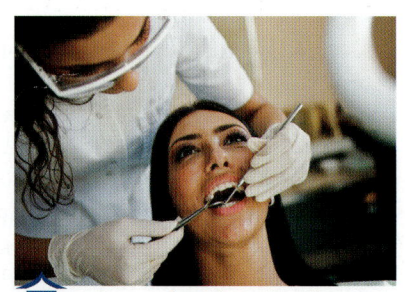

B Everyone should use dental services

Now you need to think about other services that the client is not using, but that might meet their needs. For example, an older person might need illness prevention but does not go for a flu vaccination every autumn. Another example is dental services. Everyone should use these services, but quite a lot of people do not. When you have found out about these services, you might ask your client why they do not use them. This might give you useful information about barriers to access. For example, the client might say, 'I can't afford the dentist'. This might lead you to find out whether there is any free dental care available that the client does not know about.

You should find out about what local services are available. You should use several sources of information to find these. A first step might be to use your local Yellow Pages. Searching the internet will probably give you more detail. You must make notes on what you find and also make a note of the source of the information.

Libraries, health centres and GP surgeries often have leaflets describing local services. If there are many providers of the same service locally, such as dentists or opticians, you should not list them all. Instead you could state the number within easy reach of the client and name the one the client uses.

Next you should find out who runs each service and how the service is structured locally. This means that you must find out whether it is in the statutory sector, the private sector or the voluntary sector. You should find out which organisation runs the service. You should explain how the service is structured locally and how it fits into the national structure of the organisation providing the service. Some small local voluntary organisations do not have a national structure, but most other organisations, such as the NHS, do.

When describing structure, you should not give the names of people in each post. Instead you should just give the name of the post (e.g. Head of Services for Older People). In many areas, the structure diagrams in older textbooks are no longer correct. This is mainly because of the integration of primary health care services with other community services including social services. In such cases, it is important to make clear to the reader that these services are run jointly (usually between the NHS and the city, county or borough council).

Information on these structures can be found in libraries or using the internet. Town libraries usually have information on local authority structure and services in the Reference section. When using your preferred internet search engine, it is useful to enter terms such as the name of your local authority plus 'social services', 'community services' or 'care trust'. The term 'structure chart' or 'organisation chart' might also get results. You should include information about local structures as well as how these fit into national structures (see Figure D).

Voluntary and private sector organisations have a simpler structure. Try searching the internet for 'NSPCC organisation chart' to see an example. When drawing up charts, it is sensible to include only those bits of the chart that deal with services. You can leave out directors of finance, human resources and publicity for example.

C *Libraries are a good source of information*

links

An example of an integrated services structure chart (for Southwark) can be viewed at www.southwarkpct.nhs.uk/documents/2443.pdf

5 Job roles and skills

5.1 Skills of care workers

Care worker skills

This section describes many of the skills used by care workers. Some of these skills are more important in some job roles than in others.

> **Objectives**
> Describe the range of skills used by care workers.

Knowledge

Most job roles require specialist knowledge. This comes partly through training, but partly through experience of doing the job. For example, nursery nurses need knowledge of infant physical, intellectual, emotional and social development.

Observation

Observation skills range from noticing a person's appearance and behaviour to using measuring equipment. Observation is important when working with people because it gives clues as to how a person is feeling, what might be wrong with them and what they might do in future. For example, a care assistant in a residential home observes that an elderly person is irritable or confused. The care assistant might report this because it could be a sign of illness, such as an infection.

Measurement and testing

Some job roles require the care worker to be able to use measuring apparatus and test procedures correctly. A practice nurse, for example, has to be able to measure blood pressure accurately. Apparatus might include X-ray and scanning equipment. Test procedures include screening tests for the genetically inherited disease phenylketonuria (**PKU**) and for cervical cancer. (For more about PKU, see Chapter 6, The nature of health and wellbeing, page 101.)

Data interpretation

Data interpretation is the skill of being able to decide what a set of measurements or observations means. For example, a hospital doctor looks at an X-ray image to assess the damage to a broken limb.

Record keeping

Care workers often have to keep records of a client's progress. These records must be accurate and kept up to date and will include any measurements made and treatments given. For example, hospital nurses keep a record of treatment given to patients in a ward. This treatment may include medication given by a drip.

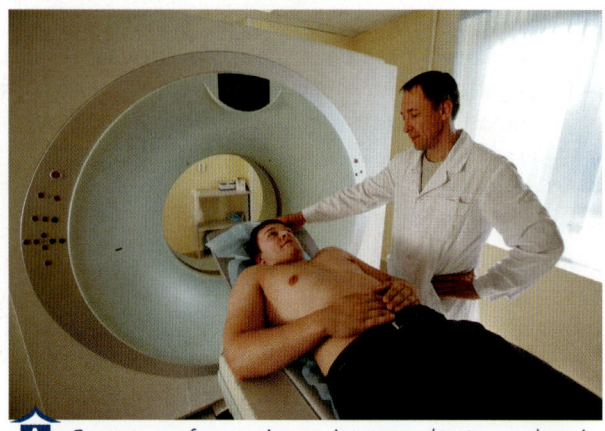

A *Correct use of measuring equipment and test procedures is another important skill*

Diagnosis

Diagnosis means using the information from observation and measurement to decide what is wrong with a person. It is a medical term. For example, a GP will use observation and blood tests to diagnose diabetes in a patient.

Treatment

Treatment is also mainly a medical term. It refers to actions taken to cure an illness or injury or to relieve symptoms. Treatment can involve particular skills, such as giving an injection or surgically removing a tumour. It also refers to things like moving and stretching a patient's arm to restore movement and placing a catheter to enable a patient to urinate.

Communication

Good communication skills are important. There are two types of communication: verbal and non-verbal.

Verbal communication

Verbal communication includes communicating in speech and by reading and writing. Some job roles require a high level of verbal skills. Some care workers have to be able to read and understand technical reports. Many care workers have to be able to write reports that are clear and accurate.

The ability to use speech effectively is also important. Care workers have to be able to speak clearly, and not only must they choose their words so that they are likely to be understood but they must also ensure that they do not offend the client. Another verbal skill is questioning. This means asking the right questions and asking them in a way the client can understand. Another very important verbal skill is listening to and understanding what other people say.

The following are examples of the use of written and spoken verbal communication skills:

- a nurse being able to read drug names and doses correctly
- a physiotherapist writing a list of suggested exercises for a client
- a care assistant in a residential home knowing whether it is appropriate to call a resident, 'Mary, love' or 'Mrs Murray'
- a pharmacist explaining to a customer what dosage of a drug to take
- a GP understanding the street names for illegal drugs that a patient says he uses.

B *Pharmacists need to be able to explain drug dosage to patients*

Non-verbal communication

Non-verbal communication means aspects of communication apart from the actual words spoken. It includes tone of voice, speed of speech, use of facial expressions, gestures, posture and eye contact. Like verbal communication, non-verbal communication involves both sending messages and attending to or receiving messages. It involves actions and observations of the other person's actions.

C *Good non-verbal communication skills are vital in many health and social care services*

The following are examples of the use of non-verbal skills:

- a nursery nurse squats down so that her face is level with an infant's; this way she can observe his facial expression and he can observe hers
- an audiologist speaks slowly and with clear movements of his lips, so that a deaf patient can understand his speech
- a nurse smiles and uses a calm tone of voice to help an anxious patient relax
- a GP makes eye contact with a patient, to try to assess whether or not she has understood him.

D Communication skills

Verbal communication	Non-verbal communication
- Writing - Reading - Speech - Listening	- Tone and speed of speech - Facial expressions - Eye contact - Posture - Gestures - Observation

Activity

Observe some non-verbal communication skills by watching part of a TV drama with the sound muted.

Information technology (IT) skills

Many care workers have to use several kinds of computer software, including word processing, database and spreadsheet applications.

The ability to do this helps with record keeping, monitoring and report writing.

Advising

Care workers often have to give advice to clients about what they should or should not do. In some jobs, giving advice is a key aspect of the role. One example is a worker at a Citizens Advice Bureau; another is an occupational therapist who advises clients with physical disabilities about aids and adaptations to make life easier.

Counselling

Counselling is a set of skills used by a range of care workers. Counselling involves getting a client to talk about their problems and paying attention to the client's verbal and non-verbal communication. It also involves feeding back to them the statements they have made. This can lead the client to a clearer understanding of the problems and what they might do about them. Counselling is not the same as giving advice. One example is a hospital nurse helping a terminally ill patient to talk about how he feels.

Modelling

Modelling means acting in an appropriate way so that a client can observe you and will copy your behaviour. It is often more effective than trying to tell a person what to do. It can be used to get people to behave in ways that are more acceptable to other people. For example, a family support worker joins in with a child's play, while parents look on.

Distraction

Distraction is a skill that is sometimes used when clients are emotionally upset, for example anxious. To distract a person is to get them to pay attention to something else. This helps them pay less attention to their pain or anxiety. For example, a dental surgery has mobiles or ceiling posters for children to look at while having dental treatment.

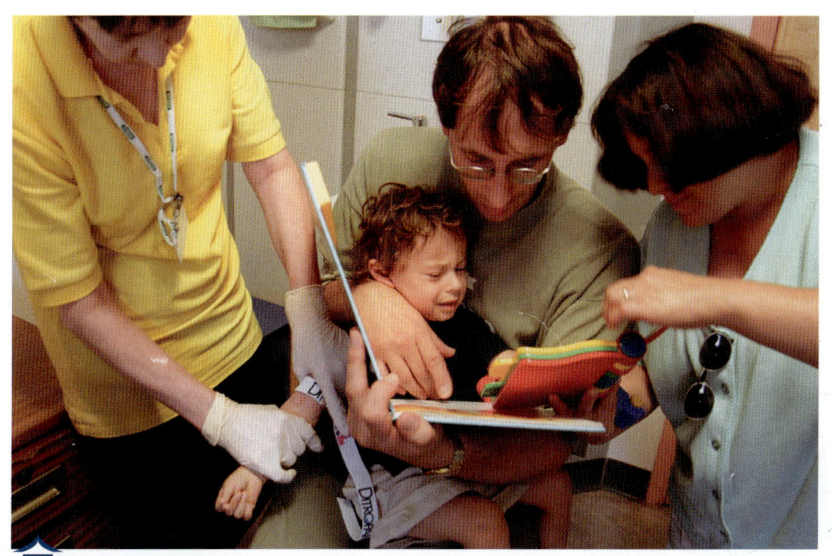

E *Distraction helps to reduce pain or distress*

Setting challenges

Setting clients a challenge can sometimes help them to gain confidence and to recover abilities lost through illness. It is a way of motivating people to improve their own skills. For example, a physiotherapist asks a stroke patient to try to walk across the room.

Educating

Some care workers need to have the skills to educate other people. Educating people means doing things that help people to learn. This can include teaching, but sometimes there are better ways of educating than teaching. One way is to set a problem or challenge for a person and then discuss it with them afterwards. Some care workers train other care workers as part of their job role. For example, a health visitor answers a parent's questions about infant care.

> **Study tip**
>
> If you are a client receiving a health or social care service, look out for staff using some of these skills. For example after you have been to the dentist note down which of these skills they used.

Assessing

Assessing means judging the quality of something. It can be used to judge how effective education has been. It can also be used to judge a person's development or needs.

One example is a social worker visiting an elderly man at home to find out how well he is able to look after himself. If he cannot look after himself properly, the social worker will arrange some help or support for him. This is called a '**needs assessment**'.

Another example is a health visitor checking the development of an eight-month-old child. This is called a '**developmental assessment**'.

Teamworking

Most care workers are part of a team. In hospitals, nurses work together with doctors, porters and health care assistants. The ability to work well in a team is important. Good **teamworking** involves communication skills, for example keeping accurate records for handing over at the end of a shift. It also involves social skills such as cooperating and preventing conflict. Another example is a medical receptionist passing on information to other staff in a GP surgery about patients who have cancelled their appointments.

F Teamworking

Leadership

Some care workers are responsible for making sure that a team of care workers are supported so that they can do their jobs properly. A care worker in this position has to act as a leader. **Leadership** requires both communication and social skills. A leader has to monitor staff working and do what is necessary to support, challenge or educate team members. Leadership can also involve deciding which staff members should do which tasks. For example, the officer in charge of a residential home plans and discusses a new shift pattern with care staff.

Monitoring

Monitoring is related to measurement, assessment and record keeping. Monitoring means checking a client's condition or progress at intervals over time. For example, a community mental health nurse regularly visits a client at home to check how he is feeling and to ensure that he is taking his medication regularly.

This is not a skill.

Aspects of personality — *quality*

Descriptions of job roles that you might find in careers books or on websites usually mention some of the skills listed above. They also often mention aspects of a personality that might help a person to do a particular care job. These are not really skills, but they probably make a difference to how well a person does a care job.

Relevant aspects of personality include being:

- caring and compassionate
- calm and patient
- able to work under pressure
- conscientious, wanting to do a job well.

G *Leadership*

5.2 Principles of care and codes of practice

Principles of care

Principles of care are a set of general guidelines for care workers. These include promoting and supporting individuals' rights to dignity, independence and health and safety.

This is really a collection of principles, including the following:

Dignity

The right to dignity means that a client should be treated respectfully. For example, washing and toileting a client should be done in private, out of view of other clients. Care workers should not make fun of clients.

Independence

This means allowing clients to do as much as possible for themselves. It is a way of empowering clients. **Empowerment** means giving people the opportunity and encouragement to do things and make decisions for themselves. For example, a nursery nurse should give an infant time to make a choice about what he will play with. A care worker should not make decisions on behalf of a client which the client could make for herself.

Health and safety

This means ensuring that clients are not exposed to unnecessary risks, such as infection or injury. For example, staff in a hospital wards should wash their hands between patients, to avoid spreading infections.

Promoting anti-discriminatory practice

Discrimination means treating people differently and unfairly, without good reason. Not taking a disabled infant on a nursery school trip to a petting zoo is discrimination on the basis of disability.

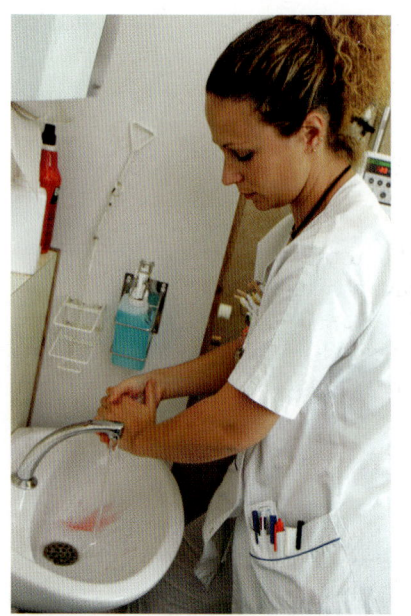

> **Objectives**
> Explain the principles of care.
> Explain how codes of practice relate to principles of care.

> **Activity**
> 1. Try to agree on a code of conduct for the students and teacher in your group at school or college. Make sure that it says what people should and should not do.

A Clients should not be exposed to unnecessary risks

Promoting **anti-discriminatory practice** means treating people fairly whatever their sex, race, religion, sexuality, disability, social class and age. It does not mean treating everybody the same. Obviously, an older person might not like to be treated in the same way as a child. A person with cancer would not want to be treated in the same way as a person with diabetes.

Maintaining confidentiality

This means keeping personal information about clients secret except from other staff who ought to have this information. In practice, it means that a client's records should be kept in a locked filing cabinet or in a password-protected electronic file. It also means that staff should not chat about clients in a public place.

Acknowledging individuals' personal beliefs and identity

This means accepting or not challenging the beliefs a client has, even if they differ from your own beliefs. An example is giving religious clients the opportunity to take part in religious acts.

Protecting individuals from abuse

This means looking out for any evidence that a person is being physically, sexually or emotionally abused and taking action to stop or prevent this. One example is taking abused children into care.

Promoting effective communication and relationships

This means trying to make sure that a client can understand what is said to them. It also means trying to understand what the client is saying. Enabling communication means that clients are less likely to be socially isolated. This might include making sure that a client's hearing aids are working or providing a translator for clients who do not speak English.

Providing individualised care

This means treating clients differently according to their different needs and preferences. It includes giving clients choices: for example, a dentist might ask a patient whether or not they would like a local anaesthetic.

■ Codes of practice, policies, procedures and employment contracts

Organisations such as the NHS, local authorities, professional organisations and voluntary organisations usually produce **codes of practice** for their members or employees. A code of practice (or conduct) applies various principles of care to a particular job role. It informs care workers of what they should and should not do.

Sometimes the same sort of information is given in the form of a set of **policies**. For example, an organisation might have a policy on discrimination, a policy on health and safety, etc. Another way in which guidance is given to care workers is through descriptions of correct procedures. In addition, employers write **employment contracts** which also tell care workers what they should and should not do.

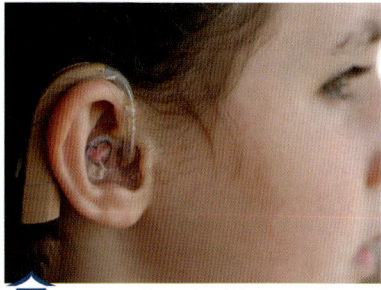

B *Care workers should ensure that a client with hearing aids can hear them properly*

Activity

2 You may have noticed that some of these principles seem to contradict each other. In practice, it is difficult to keep to all of them at the same time, as the following examples show:

a A 14-year-old boy in a wheelchair is on an activity holiday in the Lake District. He wants to go up a smooth mountain track on his own. Which principles are relevant here? What would you do if you were responsible for the boy?

b A religious Jew in hospital is offended by being asked to choose a meal from a menu, because one of the items on the menu is pork. Which principles are relevant here? What would you do?

c A child who has been taken into care is placed with a foster family but wants to go back to his own family. Which principles are relevant here? What would you do if you were the social worker in charge of the case?

5.3 Researching Assignment 2

What you have to do

In this assignment, you have to choose three different jobs in health, social care or early years. The roles could be those of providers, who are directly involved with providing care to clients, or they could be roles of support staff, whose work is not directly involved with care. For example, you might choose a GP, a hospital porter and a nursery nurse. You might want to choose one job role that you are interested in yourself. You might also choose a job role because you know someone who does this job. Note that you should write about the role, not about a particular person you know who has that role.

You should not choose any job roles that are not clearly about health, social care or early years. For example, you should not choose a secondary school teacher or a police officer. The job roles you might choose from include a wide range of care provider roles, such as a GP, nursery nurse, dietician or social worker. You could also choose support staff roles, such as a medical receptionist, cleaner or hospital porter.

Researching job roles

You should first collect and make notes on the aims, responsibilities, care actions and skills of each job role. You will find careers manuals, such as the Connexions catalogue useful. There will probably be copies of these manuals in your school or college library.

There are also useful websites describing job roles, including the careers website Connexions (see Links) and sites for particular job roles. Remember the following when you use these websites.

- You should keep a note of the web address so that you can include it in your appendix.
- You should not include information that is not relevant to this assignment. For example, don't include information about rates of pay, working hours, or training and qualifications needed.
- You should not simply copy what the website says or 'cut and paste' sections of it into your assignment. Instead, make notes of the information then write it up in your own words.

Objectives
Find and use relevant sources of information.

links
www.connexions-direct.com
www.prospects.ac.uk
www.careersadvice.direct.gov.uk
www.ccwales.org.uk
www.nhscareers.nhs.uk
www.socialworkcareers.co.uk
www.childcarecareers.gov.uk

A Make notes from your website sources and write down the web address too

You might find it useful to organise your notes on each job role into several sections:

- aims and responsibilities
- care actions
- skills.

You might also have the opportunity to talk to someone who does one of the job roles you have chosen. This could be a good source of information. However, you should also use published information (books and websites). If you cannot find out much about one of your chosen job roles, you might decide to choose a different one.

B *Researching job roles in the careers library*

Researching codes of practice

You already have a list of principles of care (see Section 5.2). You need to research the actual guidelines that care organisations give their employees. Remember that these guidelines are really principles of care applied to particular job roles.

The easiest way to research these is by using the internet. Use your preferred search engine to search, using words like 'nursing code of practice'. You might also look for particular items in the principles of care list, such as 'health and safety and childminder'. As usual, make a note of the sources you use. Different countries in the UK and different local authorities sometimes have different codes of practice.

You could look at your local authority website for codes of practice relating to social work, residential care or early years services. You will probably find it useful to write down the codes of conduct you find. If these are already in a suitable form, you can copy them from the internet. These copies should be included in the Appendix of your report.

links

www.nmc-uk.org – this gives a code of conduct for nurses and midwives

www.cdta-online.co.uk – code of conduct for dentists

www.topssengland.net – code of practice for social workers

www.caretolearn.lsc.gov.uk – code of practice for childminders

Study tip

When searching the web, make sure you use sites that refer to the UK. Otherwise it is easy to make the mistake of collecting information about care services in other English-speaking countries such as Australia, Canada or the United States.

6 The nature of health and wellbeing

6.1 Definitions of health and wellbeing

Activity

1. Before reading any further, write two sentences describing what is meant by health. You could also do this as a group exercise in which each person calls out words or phrases to complete the sentence 'Being healthy means …' Look back at what you said after reading the next section.

Objectives

Know three definitions of health and wellbeing.

Identify examples of each view of health and wellbeing.

Describe how ideas about health and wellbeing have changed over time and vary between different cultures.

Definitions of health and wellbeing

In this section, we shall look at three **definitions of health and wellbeing**.

The negative definition of health and wellbeing

The obvious answer to the question 'What is meant by being healthy?' is 'Not being ill'. This is called the **negative definition** because it is saying that there is nothing wrong with a person who is healthy. According to this definition, health is the absence of illness.

A good description of the negative view or definition is:

> Health and wellbeing is the absence of physical illness, disease and mental distress.

An example is a person not having diabetes or depression.

Most people would probably agree with this negative definiton, but there are two other possible definitions (see below).

The positive definition of health and wellbeing

The only reason we might want a different definition is if the first one was not completely right. It turns out that the negative definition is not quite right, as the following example shows.

John is a bit overweight, has an unbalanced diet and smokes cigarettes. At the moment John is not ill. But is he healthy? You could say that his lifestyle is unhealthy and is likely to make him ill sooner or later.

According to the **positive view**, health and wellbeing is not just the absence of illness. Instead, health and wellbeing is something a person has to aim at and can achieve only by some effort. According to this view, John is not healthy and could only be healthy if his lifestyle was different. He would have to start eating a balanced diet and stop smoking, for example. He would also have to do something to maintain his emotional or mental wellbeing, such as spend time with supportive friends or family members.

A *John smokes and is not ill – but is he healthy?*

A description of the positive view or definition is:

> Health and wellbeing is the achievement and maintenance of physical fitness and mental stability.

This can be achieved, for example, by taking exercise, eating a balanced diet and using leisure time to relax.

The holistic definition of health and wellbeing

A person's physical health and wellbeing can be affected by physical, intellectual, emotional and social factors:

- **Physical effects** on health include damage to the body by disease micro-organisms, such as bacteria.
- **Intellectual effects** on health include having beliefs that affect health. For example, a man who has had a heart attack might believe that he should rest all the time. The lack of exercise is likely to make his heart worse, and his wellbeing might suffer because of the lack of activity.
- **Emotional effects** on health include feeling depressed because of an illness. A woman who has been told that she has cancer might be so depressed by this that she stops taking care of herself. This could reduce her chances of getting better after having treatment for the cancer.
- **Social effects** on health include having supportive friends. A man who is off work because of illness for several weeks might feel better and improve in health if a friend visits him to cheer him up and encourages him to do the exercises suggested by his physiotherapist.

Most health workers understand that a patient's health and wellbeing is affected not only by what is physically wrong with the body, but also by the person's beliefs, feelings and social contacts. This means that they have a holistic view of health and wellbeing. 'Holistic' means 'including everything'.

A description of the holistic view or definition is:

> Health and wellbeing is the continuation of the result of a combination of physical, intellectual, emotional and social factors.

This can mean, for example, being physically fit and well, intellectually alert, without negative emotions and with plenty of supportive friends.

Summary table for revision

C *Definitions or views of health and wellbeing*

Negative	Health and wellbeing is the absence of illness and mental distress
Positive	Health and wellbeing is the achievement and maintenance of physical fitness and mental stability
Holistic	Health and wellbeing is the result of a combination of physical, social, intellectual and emotional factors (PIES)

Activity

2 Now look back at what you said about health and wellbeing in the first activity. Decide which of the words or phrases relate more to a negative definition and which relate more to a positive definition.

B Too much rest can be unhealthy, even after a heart attack

Study tip

You should learn all three definitions. You should also be able to **describe** each of these three views. You can do this by giving each definition with an example.

Study tip

Try practice question 1 at the end of this chapter (page 126).

Changing ideas of health and wellbeing

Views about health and wellbeing change over time, and also differ from culture to culture. Here are some examples.

The four humour theory

In Europe until around the 18th century, the usual explanation for disease was the **four humour theory**. The humours were based on liquids found in the body. These were black bile, yellow bile, phlegm and blood. The theory said that disease was caused by too much or too little of one or other of these. For a person to be healthy, the humours had to be in balance. Treating disease was done by trying to change the amount of whichever humour was lacking or was present in excess. For example, too much blood could cause some diseases. The treatment for these was to take blood from the patient, sometimes by using leeches, sometimes by 'cupping'. Cupping used a vacuum to suck blood out. Today, people understand that this theory is not correct. Taking blood from a person who is ill is likely to make them worse. The treatments based on the four humour theory were probably either harmful to health or not effective at all.

D *A doctor bleeding a patient*

Germ theory

From 1850 to around 1900, the **germ theory** was developed. The germ theory said that infectious diseases were spread by tiny microorganisms, invisible to the naked eye. Among the first infectious microorganisms to be discovered were bacteria, which can easily be seen under a microscope. These were first observed in 1676, but the connection with infections was not made until the next century. Later, much smaller microorganisms called viruses were discovered. There is plenty of evidence that this theory is largely correct.

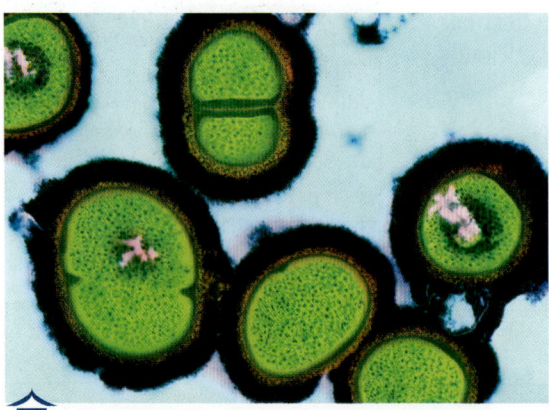

E *We now know that bacteria can spread disease*

Shamanism and spiritual beliefs

In some cultures, people believe that diseases are caused by evil spirits. The treatment of diseases is carried out by people who have both a religious and a healing role. They are called shamans. For example, among Indian groups in South America, shamans cast out evil spirits, using powerful herbs and religious ritual.

F *Casting out 'evil spirits'*

The belief in spirits has probably existed for much of human prehistory. Because many diseases do not have visible causes, spiritual explanations were widely believed. The result of such beliefs was sometimes extremely cruel treatment. A person with a mental disorder might be beaten or burned to death to get rid of the evil spirits.

Ancient skulls found in various parts of the world show holes that are the result of healed trepanning wounds. Trepanning is cutting a hole in a living person's skull. Today, it is used in brain surgery. In pre-history, without anaesthetics or antiseptics, it would have been a very dangerous operation. It is possible that some of these ancient skulls were trepanned to release evil spirits.

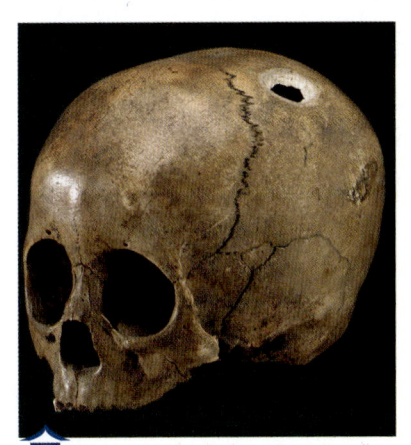

G *Trepanning may have been used to release the evil spirits that were believed to cause illness*

Recent religious explanations

In the 1980s, **HIV/AIDS** was a relatively new disease. Some Christian conservatives in the USA explained AIDS as a punishment by God for homosexual acts. AIDS was called a 'gay plague'. In fact, the cause of HIV/AIDS is a virus. HIV can affect people regardless of their sexuality. Today, people in Britain understand that infectious disease such as flu and pneumonia are caused by microorganisms, not by gods or evil spirits.

6.2 Factors affecting health – regular exercise

Factors affecting health

Meanwhile...

... in Ramsay MacDonald Street ...

Jasmeena Aziz is serving at the post office counter, while Juliet Webster vacuum cleans the stairs in the house behind the shop. Jasmeena notices that the noise of the vacuum cleaner has stopped and that there is no sound from Juliet. She suspects that Juliet has stopped to have a cigarette, even though Jasmeena has asked her not to smoke in the house. Jasmeena asks Nazir to mind the counter while she goes to investigate. She finds Juliet sitting on the stairs, very out of breath. She makes her a cup of tea. 'Did you remember to have your insulin injection this morning?' she asks. Juliet says that she did but adds that she is often very short of breath. 'I'm just unlucky, I suppose,' says Juliet. 'Some people twice my age have nothing wrong with them. And here's me with high blood pressure, heart failure, bad knees and I don't know what else. It never rains but it pours.' Jasmeena says, 'I don't think it's anything to do with the weather. Perhaps you've done too much. Go home now and lie down.'

A

> **Objectives**
>
> Explain the benefits of regular exercise.
>
> Describe the health problems resulting from lack of exercise.
>
> Explain the importance of exercise at different life stages.

> **Study tip**
>
> You should understand the **positive** and **negative** health effects of these factors and also how they affect people at the different life stages, i.e. infancy, childhood, adolescence, adulthood and later adulthood.

The rest of this chapter is about factors that positively or negatively affect a person's health and wellbeing. Some of these are **lifestyle factors**, which can be controlled by people themselves. For example, a person can decide on how much exercise they have or what they eat and drink.

Other factors are less easy for people to control. For example, people have no control over their own genetic make-up. They can do nothing to affect whether or not they have a genetic disease. People might also find it hard to control social and economic factors, such as how much money they have or whether or not they have a job. Individuals might not be able to control environmental factors such as pollution.

B *You have control over how much you eat and drink*

Regular exercise

Exercise means intentional physical activity. Exercise is a physical factor. It is one of the lifestyle factors over which people can have control. For example, most people can choose to go for a walk, go swimming, play sports and join in physical training. Gym facilities include equipment designed to exercise a wide range of muscle groups and are suitable for people of very different levels of fitness.

Regular exercise can positively contribute to health in different ways.

Exercise can keep joints, muscles and bones healthy

Our muscles and the joints between our bones (e.g. a knee joint) enable us to move. As long as we keep using these, they are likely to stay healthy.

C *The effects of exercise and lack of exercise on joints, muscles and bones*

	Effects of exercise	Effects of lack of exercise
Joint flexibility	Maintains flexibility, e.g. the ability to bend double or raise the arms above the head	Lack of flexibility, e.g. not being able to kneel down fully
Mobility	Maintains mobility, enabling us to move about by walking, running, etc.	Reduction or loss of mobility, e.g. not being able to climb stairs
Strength	Muscles stay strong or get stronger if they are used regularly	Reduction in strength, e.g. being too weak to stand up
Stamina	Maintains the ability to keep moving for long periods, e.g. walking 20 miles	Low stamina – getting tired easily
Bone growth	Regular exercise that involves stressing or shocking the bones improves bone growth; examples include using a trampoline, running, ball games and skateboarding	Reduced bone growth, which can lead to brittle bones in later adulthood, especially in women; this condition is called **osteoporosis**

D *Exercise can keep body systems healthy*

Exercise can keep the circulatory system healthy

The **circulatory system** includes the heart, the blood and the blood vessels. Blood vessels are tough tubes running to all parts of the body. These include the arteries and veins, which are quite thick, but there are also lots of very narrow tubes. The main purpose of the circulatory system is to get oxygen and food energy to body organs, such as the brain and muscles. It also takes waste products, such as carbon dioxide, away from these organs. These chemicals are carried along in the blood.

The heart is a powerful pump that pushes the blood through the blood vessels. It pumps by sucking blood in and then pushing it out in a pulse. It does this about 70 times every minute. This is the average **pulse rate**. To get enough oxygen and food to all the organs in the body, the heart has to pump quite hard. This means that **blood pressure** has to be quite high. When a person is standing up, the pressure has to be high enough to pump blood up to the brain. It also has to be high enough to force blood back up from the legs to the heart.

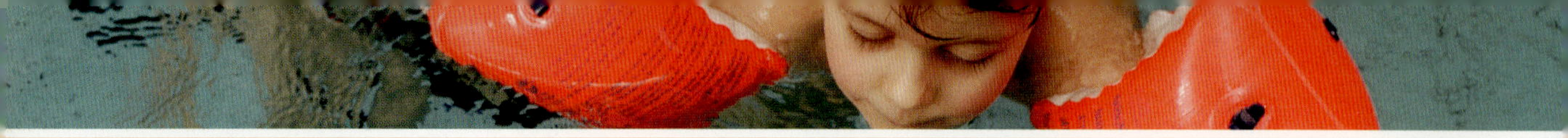

A person who is fit and healthy will show a range of blood pressures. When the person is taking exercise (e.g. running uphill), blood pressure will be high. This is because the muscles are using a lot of food and oxygen. This high blood pressure is not a risk to health unless the person continues too long, or tries too hard. When the person rests, the blood pressure will reduce again.

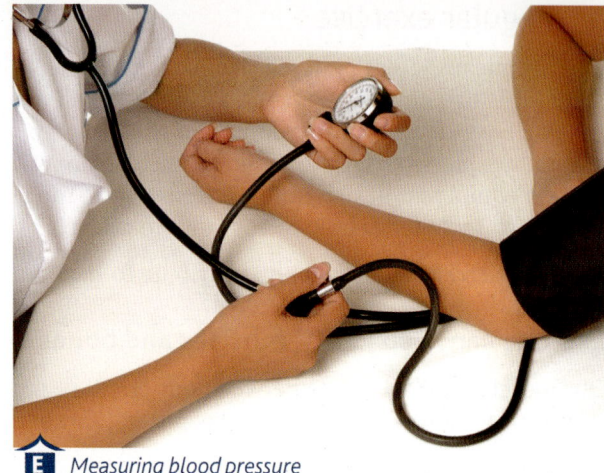

Exercise is good for health partly because it causes changes in blood pressure. Changes in demand on the body make it more able to cope with demands in future. Stressing the circulatory system does it good. Exercise keeps the circulatory system working efficiently.

E Measuring blood pressure

Lack of exercise can make the circulatory system work less well. People who take little or no exercise are more likely to have a higher than normal blood pressure most of the time. The heart has to work quite hard even when the person is at rest. This constant high blood pressure is called **hypertension**. It is a form of illness, but it does not show symptoms. People with hypertension are often unaware that they have a problem.

There is always a risk that a system with fluid under pressure will leak. It happens with central heating radiators and bicycle tyres. If you accidentally cut yourself, you usually puncture some of the smaller blood vessels and blood leaks out. Blood can also leak inside the body, for example into joints or into the brain.

The blood contains substances that quickly act to mend these punctures. These include clotting factors, which make the blood turn solid. On a cut, this forms a scab that stops the leak and helps the cut to heal.

If a person's blood pressure is high most of the time, the risk of leaks is increased. This can lead to **strokes** where blood leaks inside the brain and causes brain damage. Hypertension also increases the risk of heart disease, because the heart continually has to work hard. Hypertension can also damage the kidneys. Most of this damage cannot be reversed. If hypertension is diagnosed early, people can receive advice and treatment for it. The best advice is to start taking gentle exercise and gradually build up.

Heart disease

Heart disease usually means **coronary artery disease**. The coronary arteries go around the outside of the heart. Their job is to supply the heart muscle itself with blood. The heart muscle must have a good supply of food energy and oxygen to keep pumping. Coronary artery disease is a narrowing of the arteries, usually because of a build-up of fats including **cholesterol** on the inside of the artery walls. This makes the arteries narrower, so they carry less blood. If the blood supply is very poor, this means that the heart cannot pump very strongly. This is called **heart failure**. Heart failure is a weakly pumping heart. The result is that the person feels tired or breathless and cannot do strenuous activity.

A **heart attack** is caused by a blood clot getting stuck in one of the coronary arteries. This is most likely to happen in people who already have narrow arteries caused by coronary artery disease. The blood clot means that the blood supply to some of the heart muscle is stopped. This soon causes the death of some of the muscle. This is one cause of heart failure. A person having a heart attack might feel dizzy and sweaty and have pain in the chest or arm. In some cases, the attack causes so much damage that the heart stops, causing death.

Taking regular exercise reduces the risk of this sort of disease. Lack of exercise increases the risk.

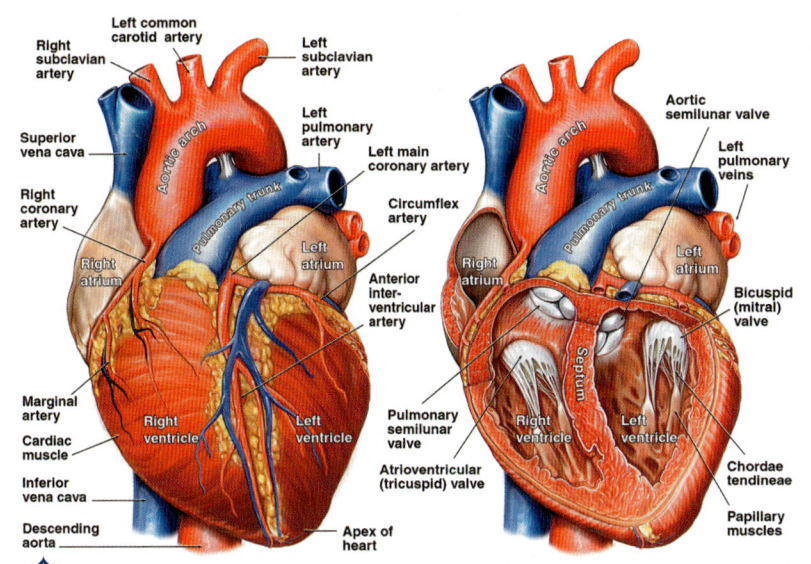

F The **coronary arteries** supply the heart muscle with blood

Exercise can keep the respiratory system healthy

The **respiratory system** includes the **lungs** and the **airways** from the nose and mouth to the lungs. The lungs allow oxygen from the air to dissolve into our blood. The blood is then pumped by the heart to all parts of the body so as to supply oxygen to organs. The oxygen is used in chemical reactions which keep the body going. In these reactions waste carbon dioxide is produced, and this is released by the lungs and breathed out. The respiratory system also depends on the strength of muscles in the chest and belly. We take a breath by using muscles to expand the space in the chest. This sucks air in.

Vigorous exercise such as running, or cycling uphill, stresses the respiratory system. This improves **lung function**. During vigorous exercise, we usually get out of breath and breathe fast and deeply. This helps to keep the system in good working order. The respiratory system can only work well if the circulatory system is in good health. Lack of exercise can lead to a loss of lung volume, as the muscles in the chest and belly are less able to suck in air.

G Cycling uphill improves lung function

Exercise can help us control our weight

Exercise uses up chemical energy (kilocalories) from the food we eat. If we do not use up this energy, the food is stored as fat. If a person has a normal diet but does little or no exercise, they are likely to gain weight. Regular exercise is a good method of **weight control**. A person who is obese (extremely overweight) is at risk of developing heart disease, hypertension, diabetes and joint problems.

Diabetes

People with diabetes usually have too much sugar in the blood. This is often because they do not produce enough of the hormone insulin, which helps to process sugars in the body. People with diabetes usually have to take extra insulin by daily injections. A test of blood sugar can indicate whether or not a person has diabetes.

Diabetes can cause damage to the eyes, nerves and kidneys, as well as causing heart attacks, strokes, hypertension and heart failure.

Exercise can improve wellbeing

Exercise can improve a person's emotional wellbeing by giving them a feeling of satisfaction and achievement. It can also help indirectly because it helps build muscles and control weight, which can improve a person's body image. Exercise can improve a person's social wellbeing because some activities involve groups or teams of people.

In contrast, a lack of exercise can increase the risk of depression and reduce self-esteem.

H Exercise can improve self-esteem

■ Exercise in the different life stages

Infancy

Infants are usually physically active in play. They do not need any additional exercise.

Childhood

Children are also typically very active and unlikely to need additional exercise. One exception is a child whose diet has led them to become overweight. For this child, exercise might be more difficult and less appealing. For example, an overweight child might be discouraged by her inability to run as fast as her peers.

Adolescence

Adolescents who are good at sports, and who have friends who take regular exercise, tend to exercise frequently. For example, they might go mountain biking and surfing with their friends. They might also be members of school sports teams, which train regularly. Exercise that stresses or shocks the bones is important in this stage, especially in girls, because it improves bone growth and reduces the risk of osteoporosis in later adulthood.

Adolescents who are less good at sports and who have parents and friends who take little exercise are more likely to take less exercise than they did as children. For them, exercise might be unrewarding, not enjoyable and 'uncool'.

I Exercise that stresses the bones is important for adolescent girls

Adulthood

In early adulthood, pressures of full-time work and child rearing can make it difficult to find time to take exercise. Even adults who took part in sport at school tend to take much less exercise. In this way, some adults lose the habit of exercising. Regular exercise at fixed times in the week, such as gym sessions or aerobics classes, can help adults to make a habit of exercise.

Later adulthood

During later adulthood, there is usually a reduction in a person's strength, mobility, flexibility and stamina. Older people sometimes do less exercise because of pain and discomfort in joints. Another reason is that physical activity is more risky in older people. For example, a simple fall that would not hurt a child or adult could lead to a broken bone in an older person. However, continuing to take exercise can help to keep joints and muscles working.

Summary table for revision

Effects of exercise and lack of exercise

PIES	Effects of exercise	Effects of lack of exercise
Effects on physical health	<ul><li>Improved flexibility, mobility, strength and stamina</li><li>Improved bone growth</li><li>Reduced or normal blood pressure</li><li>Improved lung function</li><li>Normal weight or body mass</li></ul>	<ul><li>Reduced flexibility, mobility, strength and stamina</li><li>Risk of osteoporosis</li><li>Hypertension</li><li>Risk of heart disease</li><li>Risk of stroke</li><li>Overweight or obesity, causing risk of diabetes</li></ul>
Effects on intellectual development	There are no significant effects	
Effects on emotional wellbeing	<ul><li>Improved body image</li><li>Improved self-esteem</li><li>Feeling of satisfaction</li><li>Sense of achievement</li><li>Feelings of contentment or satisfaction</li><li>An enjoyable leisure activity</li></ul>	<ul><li>Reduced body image</li><li>Reduced self-esteem</li><li>Boredom</li></ul>
Effects on social wellbeing	<ul><li>Wider social circle</li></ul>	

Activities

1. Now re-read the description of Juliet's 'funny turn' on page 82.
   a. List all the things that are wrong with Juliet's physical health.
   b. Juliet thinks she is unlucky to have several things wrong with her at the same time. Is there a reason why she has this combination of diseases?
2. Re-read the description of Bob's 'funny turn' on page 6. What do you think was wrong with Bob?

Study tip

Try practice question 2 at the end of this chapter (page 126).

6.3 Factors affecting health – diet

Diet and health

Meanwhile... ... in Ramsay MacDonald Street ...

Naomi Webster is at Katya's house one evening. Katya thinks Naomi is upset about something. They listen as Magda sings a Polish nursery rhyme.

'Doesn't she get mixed up?' asks Naomi. 'How does she know what language to talk?' 'It's not a problem,' replies Katya. 'They pick up languages easily at her age. When Tomasz is home we speak Polish all the time, except when there are visitors. That would not be polite, I think.'

'So did you grow up speaking English and Polish?' asks Naomi. 'No, I grew up speaking Polish and Russian,' says Katya. 'I learned English only later, in school. That's why it is sometimes not so good. Now tell me, what's the trouble?' Naomi looks at her, and tears well up in her eyes. 'I'm fat, and there's nothing I can do about it. Mum says it's just puppy fat, and that I'll grow out of it, but I won't. What do you think?'

'Yes, you are too fat,' says Katya. 'It is good you understand that. So what are you going to do about it?'

Naomi describes what had happened yesterday evening. For a week, she had been trying to eat less. She wanted to stop eating sweets, biscuits, bread and fried foods. When she chose salads for lunch at school, her friends teased her. When she came home from school yesterday, her mother gave her bacon, eggs, sausage and fried bread for tea. Naomi had refused to eat it and had yoghurt and some fruit. That evening she felt hungrier and hungrier. The television advertisements were mostly about food. Later on, her mother had said, 'I'm hungry again. Why don't we treat ourselves?' Naomi was sent up the street to MacRamsay's takeaway for a big order of chicken gobbets and chips. Back home, her mother had said, 'Eat something. Naomi; you can't live on fresh air.' Naomi had ended up eating a whole bucket of chips herself. Later, she tried to make herself sick, but failed.

'This making yourself sick is very bad. It is not the way. Otherwise, you tried to do the right thing,' said Katya. 'But things were against you. When all the family eat like that it is difficult to be different.' 'It's Mum's fault I'm fat,' says Naomi. 'She's brought me up eating too much of the wrong food, and when I try to eat properly she won't back me up. If it hadn't been for her, I would never have ate them chips.'

'What good does it do to blame?' asks Katya. 'Instead, think how to put things right. You still want to lose weight?' 'Yes,' sobs Naomi. Katya gives Naomi some advice.

A

Objectives

Define a balanced diet.

Name food components.

Explain the benefits of a balanced diet and the health risks of an unbalanced or inadequate diet.

Explain how a balanced diet changes in different life stages.

Diet is another physical factor. It is also a lifestyle factor, because people can usually choose what and how much they eat and drink. Most of the information you need on diet is in Chapter 3, Influencing factors starting on page 46. You should read and revise this.

Food preparation and health

The way food is prepared can also have an effect on health. For example, foods that are fried in oils often include high levels of fat. Grilling or steaming food does not increase its fat content.

Effects of diet on wellbeing

The food available in Britain today is better tasting and more attractive than ever before. Eating and drinking are ways in which people indirectly control their moods. Most people feel more content and happier after a delicious meal.

One result of this is that, when people feel unhappy, they are often tempted to improve their mood by eating. This is called 'comfort eating'. While this has an immediate positive effect on mood, it can have a long-term negative effect on health, as it leads to an unbalanced diet.

Diet in different life stages

Infancy

From birth, the best diet for an infant is breast milk. For the infant, this is a balanced diet. Breast milk contains a near perfect balance of fats, carbohydrates (mainly sugars), proteins, vitamins and minerals. It is best for an infant because it contains the combination of food components that enable the very fast growth that happens in infancy. The same combination of food components would not be suitable for adults, who are no longer growing. Breast milk might also help infants to resist infections. Not all infants are breastfed.

Gradually, infants can be weaned from a milk-only diet to a diet that also includes some solid foods. This enables the child to eat a wider variety of foods, including fruits and vegetables.

B *Breast milk provides a balanced diet for a young infant*

Childhood

Children continue to grow, so they need a diet rich in protein, vitamins and minerals. Because they are larger, they will need more of each food component than they did when younger. They will also need carbohydrates and fats to make up for the energy they use in exercise and play.

Children often only like a narrow range of foods, especially foods high in sugars. This can make it difficult to ensure that a child's diet is balanced. Parents sometimes make the mistake of letting children eat as much as they want of foods high in fats and carbohydrates. This can lead to obesity within a few years. There is evidence that obesity in childhood makes it much harder for a person to control their weight for the rest of their lives.

Adolescence

Adolescents continue to grow, so they also need a diet rich in protein, vitamins and minerals. Because they are larger, they will need more of each food component than they did when younger. After puberty, girls need a higher intake of iron. Iron is an ingredient of blood, which the body has to replace after some is lost by menstruation. This means that a balanced diet for adolescent girls will contain more iron than is required in a balanced diet for boys.

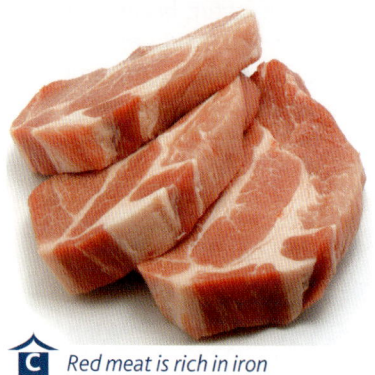

C Red meat is rich in iron

Some adolescents who are worried about their body image choose to have an inadequate diet, with not enough of several food components. This can lead to weight loss and ill health.

Adulthood

People tend to become less and less active as they go through adulthood. This means that their requirements for food energy get less. Therefore, they should eat less food containing fat and carbohydrate. In fact, people usually continue to eat the same amount over time, so adults often gain weight as they get older.

Pregnant women have an extra requirement for proteins, vitamins and minerals. They might not need more fats and carbohydrates because pregnancy itself can lead to a reduction in physical activity.

Overweight adults are less mobile than others and can have difficulty in taking exercise, which means that they require less food energy and should eat less than people who take exercise. 'Going on a diet' is not necessarily a good way to lose weight. One problem with dieting is that people spend a lot of time thinking about food – which makes them feel hungrier. A more effective method of weight control is to take frequent gentle exercise (e.g. swimming). It is also useful to avoid situations that encourage eating, such as watching cookery programmes or advertisements for food on TV.

D Sometimes going on a diet means you spend too much time thinking about food!

Later adulthood

Older people tend to have smaller appetites and their stomachs are less elastic than in the previous stage. This leads to some reduction in food intake. At the same time, older people often become less active, so that they do not lose weight. People with mobility problems tend to gain weight because of the lack of exercise.

Chapter 6 The nature of health and wellbeing

Summary table for revision

E *Food components and physical health*

Food component	Foods containing this component	Effects on physical health Positive	Effects on physical health Negative
Carbohydrate	Sugar, cakes, bread, rice, potatoes, pasta, cereals	Provides food energy	Excess food energy is stored as fat – risk of obesity, diabetes, heart disease, hypertension. Sugary foods can lead to tooth decay
Fibre/NSP	Wholemeal bread, oats, peas, beans	Aids digestion, prevents constipation	No major problems
Fat	Cooking oil, butter, margarine, bacon, cheese, nuts	Provides food energy. Provides heat insulation	Raised cholesterol level causes heart disease. Excess fat can cause obesity, diabetes, heart disease, hypertension
Protein	Meat, fish, eggs, milk cheese, peas, beans	Growth and repair of cells. Provides food energy	No major problems
Minerals	Meat, liver, eggs, milk, vegetables, fruit	Cell growth. Prevent deficiency diseases	Excess sodium chloride (salt) can cause hypertension
Vitamins	Meat, liver, fish, milk, vegetables, fruit	Help body chemistry. Prevent deficiency diseases	Excess vitamin supplements can be toxic
Water	Drinks, vegetables, fruit	Is needed for body fluids, e.g. blood, and for lubricating joints	No major problems

Activity

1 Now re-read the description of Naomi's chat with Katya on page 88.
  a Which was the main food component Naomi tried to cut down on?
  b Why did Naomi want to avoid fried foods? Which food component is always present in these foods?
  c How did Naomi's relationships interfere with her attempt to change her diet?
  d What advice do you think Katya should give to Naomi?
  e Katya was a source of support for Naomi. Give two ways in which she helped.

Study tip
Try practice question 3 at the end of this chapter (page 126).

6.4 Factors affecting health – substance misuse

Substance misuse and health

Substance misuse is another physical factor that can negatively influence health and wellbeing. The substances referred to in this section are tobacco, alcohol, solvents, illegal recreational drugs, and legal over-the-counter and prescribed medical drugs. The use of most of these is a lifestyle factor, which people can have control over.

> **Objectives**
> Describe different types of substance misuse.
>
> Describe the health effects of substance misuse.

Meanwhile...

... in Ramsay MacDonald Street ...

Nazir Aziz has had back pain for nearly a year. His GP prescribed some tablets called dihydrocodeine, which reduced the pain, so that Nazir could sleep at night. When Nazir finished the course of tablets, he went to his GP again, complaining that the pain had returned. The pain was not nearly as bad, but it seemed to make Nazir irritable, itchy and restless. The GP gave him a prescription for a further supply of the same tablets. Nazir continues to take them and is not usually troubled by pain.

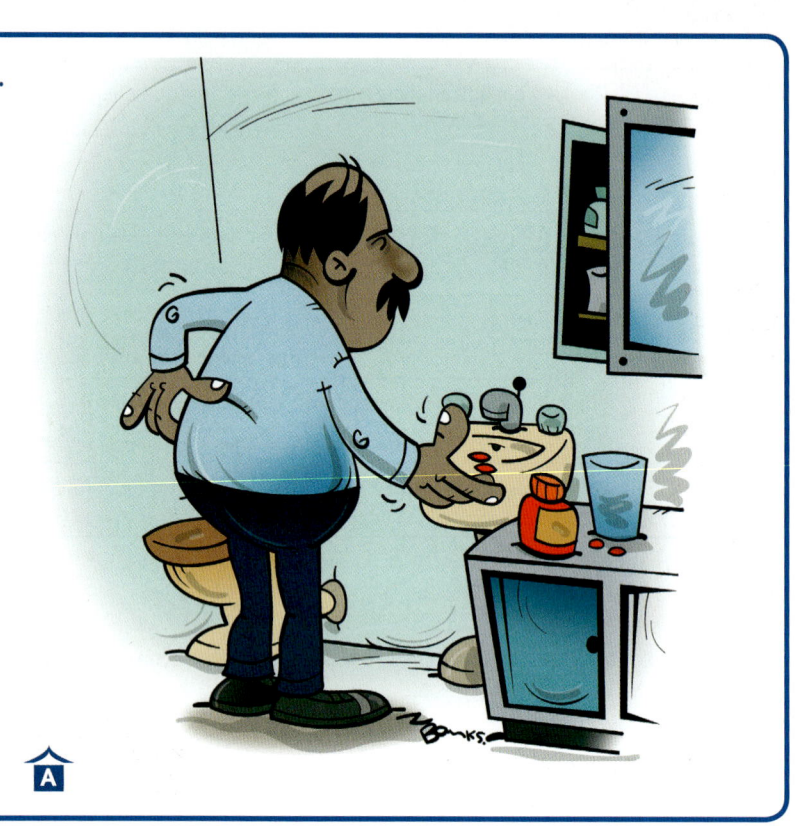

A

Substances that are misused

Tobacco

Smoking tobacco causes **lung cancer** and other respiratory illnesses such as **bronchitis**. It is also a major cause of mouth and throat cancer. Smoking during pregnancy increases the risk that infants will be stillborn, or have a low birth weight. Smoking increases the risk of hypertension, strokes, coronary heart disease and heart attacks. Smoking can also cause the skin to become wrinkled, and it can lead to an early menopause in women.

These risks are much greater for people who smoke very often. Giving up smoking reduces the risk. For some people, smoking becomes an **addiction**, which makes it much harder for them to give up.

Alcohol

Alcohol is misused in two ways.

Binge drinking

Binge drinking means drinking much more than the recommended limit of alcohol on a particular occasion. The government recommends that men should not regularly drink more than three or four units of alcohol per day, and women not more than two or three units a day. After heavy drinking (i.e. more than the recommended limit), you should not drink alcohol for 48 hours.

One pint of beer, lager or cider is between one and one and a half units, depending on its strength. One small glass of wine is one unit. A standard glass is one and a half units. A single shot of spirits is one unit, although some bars serve shots that contain one and a half to two units. This means that the recommended limit per day for men is between two and three pints of beer or glasses of wine or shots of spirits. The recommended limit for women is two pints of beer or glasses of wine or spirits.

Alcoholism

Alcoholism means addiction to alcohol, in which the person drinks excessively on most days of the week. Typically, the person tries to conceal this from other people.

Excessive drinking causes drunkenness. This is a state in which a person's judgment and reaction speed are reduced. A person who is drunk is much more likely to have an accident, such as a fall, than they are if they were sober. Drunkenness can lead to a lack of ability to control the expression of emotion. As a result, fighting happens much more among people who are drunk.

Excessive alcohol misuse can lead to inflammation of the liver. If this is continued over a long period, the liver is permanently damaged. This is called **cirrhosis**; it is eventually fatal and there is no cure. Alcohol is a major cause of cancers of the mouth and throat.

B *Alcohol and tobacco are both addictive and both can cause cancers*

Alcohol misuse can also cause hypertension and strokes. Damage to nerve cells can also occur, leading to numbness and pain, muscle weakness and memory loss. Alcohol is addictive, which makes it hard for people who regularly drink heavily to give up.

Solvents

Solvents include cigarette lighter fuel and chemicals used in some glues and aerosols. Breathing in solvents while working can cause dizziness, leading to accidents. For example, this can happen when spray-painting in a room without much ventilation. Solvent misuse is intentionally breathing in these substances. In addition to accidents, solvent abuse can cause death by stopping the heart. It can also cause liver disease and can permanently damage the lungs.

Illegal drugs

Illegal drugs are those which it is illegal to own, buy or sell. Illegal drugs include ecstasy, cannabis, heroin, cocaine and crack cocaine. Different illegal drugs have different effects on health. For example, smoking cannabis is a risk factor for cancers, although not as great a risk as smoking tobacco. Drugs such as ecstasy can cause brain damage, while cocaine and crack can cause depression, anxiety and brain damage.

Legal drugs

Most people are aware of the risks of consuming alcohol, tobacco and illegal drugs. In contrast, few people realise that patients sometimes misuse prescription drugs. If a GP prescribes a painkiller or anti-anxiety drug, the patient is likely to assume that the drug is not one which can be misused. The result is that the patient might become addicted without realising it.

Taken in large amounts over a long period, some legal drugs can cause kidney failure.

C *Some people smoke cannabis, which is an illegal drug*

Substance misuse in different life stages

Infancy and childhood

Substance misuse is rare in these life stages. However, the effects of having parents who misuse substances can be severe, including neglect and physical abuse.

Adolescence

Adolescence is the life stage in which many people start drinking alcohol. It is also a common age for taking up smoking and for trying out exciting-sounding illegal drugs. Adolescents are often strongly influenced by their peers, who might have a culture that supports substance misuse.

Adulthood

During adulthood, there is a tendency to continue some of the substance misuse habits that developed during adolescence. This might be because the person has become addicted. Some adults reduce their misuse of substances as they become older.

D *Adolescents are often influenced by their peers*

Later adulthood

In adulthood and later adulthood, it becomes more and more likely that people will become ill and need medical treatment. At this stage, a person is at more risk of misusing medical drugs. For example, a person who has been taking anti-anxiety drugs prescribed by a GP might become dependent on them. They might believe that if they stop taking the drugs they will feel worse. This makes them anxious about not having the drug, so the GP continues to prescribe it.

Summary table for revision

E *Effects of substance misuse on physical health*

Substance	Effects on physical health
Tobacco	Cancers, bronchitis, hypertension, strokes, heart disease, addiction
Alcohol	Liver disease, cirrhosis, hypertension, strokes, cancers, nerve damage, addiction, accidents
Solvents – glues, aerosols, butane	Heart stopping, lung damage, liver disease, accidents
Illegal drugs – cannabis, cocaine, etc.	Depression, anxiety, brain damage, addiction
Legal drugs – painkillers, anti-anxiety drugs	Kidney damage, addiction

Activities

1. Re-read the description of Nazir on page 92. Explain why Nazir should try to cut down his uses of painkillers, and eventually stop taking them.

2. Three other people (Ramsay MacDonald Street neighbours or their relatives) have also suffered ill-health effects because of substance abuse. Find out who these three people are and in each case name the substances abused and the health effects on the person.
Hint: don't forget about the very youngest of the neighbours.

Study tip

Try practice question 4 at this end of this chapter (page 126).

6.5 Factors affecting health – unprotected sex

Unprotected sex and health

> **Objectives**
> Define unprotected sex.
> Describe several sexually transmitted infections.

Meanwhile...

... in Ramsay MacDonald Street ...

Katya is in the park, playing with Magda on the swings, when she sees Zena walking past. She calls out, 'Hi, Zena, didn't you see me?' Zena rushes up to Katya and clutches her arm. 'The most terrible thing has happened,' she says. Her eyes are red. Zena tells Katya about her boyfriend, Colin, who lives on the other side of town. Colin is 18 years old and goes to the same school as Zena. He is tall and handsome and is captain of the school football team.

A

'You kept this a secret, didn't you?' says Katya. 'I didn't want Mum to find out,' replies Zena. 'She thinks I'm too young to have boyfriends. And, anyway, she wouldn't like Colin.'

'How long has he been your boyfriend?' asks Katya. 'Only a few days, really. We got chatting in the library at school. At first I couldn't believe he was interested in me, but it turned out that we like the same bands and think the same way. Amazing really.' Katya is beginning to form an impression of Colin, but a rather different one from Zena's.

'He took me out in his car, because we couldn't meet at my place or his parents' place. We watched the sun going down from the car park at the top of Beacon Hill. He told me he loved me, and I said I loved him. Then we had sex.' Katya is shocked. 'You did what?' 'I know it was a mistake, now,' says Zena. 'But it seemed right at the time. When he said he loved me it felt like we had got engaged. He was so romantic. And I thought most of the other girls in my class have had sex. I thought if I said no the moment would pass and I'd regret it for the rest of my life.'

'Is that true, about most of the other girls in your class?' asks Katya. 'I thought it was, but now I'm not sure. I think some of them were just pretending,' says Zena. 'Did he use a condom?' asks Katya. 'Yes, he did. Some of the time,' replies Zena. 'Some of the time is no use,' says Katya. 'You could still catch an infection, or even get pregnant. Does he have sex with other girls?'

'When he said he loved me, I just thought there couldn't be anyone else. But I saw him just now in the town centre. He had his arm round another girl. He didn't see me. That's where I've come from.'

Zena bursts into tears, and Katya gives her a hug. Magda clings to their legs.

Most people have control over their sexual behaviour, so this is another physical lifestyle factor. Choice of sexual partners, whether or not to have sex and whether or not to have unprotected sex are lifestyle choices.

Unprotected sex means a sex act in which a condom is not used to prevent or reduce contact with a partner's body fluids. These sex acts are likely to involve contact between the penis and vagina, but sex acts can also include anal sex (in which the penis enters the anus) and oral sex (contact between one partner's mouth and the other partner's genitals).

Unprotected sex is most likely to be a health risk if one of the partners has a **sexually transmitted infection** (STI). It can also be a health risk if the woman becomes pregnant, because pregnancy itself increases health risks to women.

Your risk of getting an STI is increased if you have several sexual partners. One reason is that you can have an STI without symptoms appearing for a while. You do not know you are infected. If you continue to have sex and do not use a condom, your partners are likely to get infected. If they also have several sexual partners, the infection can spread rapidly in a population.

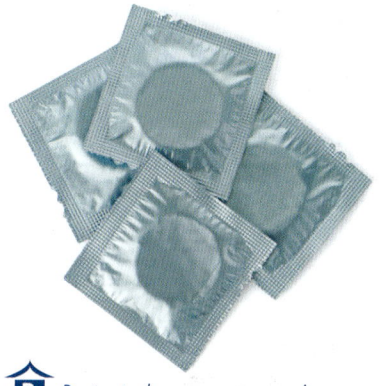

If one partner in a sex act has an STI, using a condom will give some protection to the other partner. For example, if a man with HIV has sex using a condom with a partner, who does not have HIV, the partner is protected from HIV. If a woman with gonorrhoea has sex with a man, who does not have the disease, the man is protected from gonorrhoea if he uses a condom. Using a condom reduces but does not completely remove the risk of infection.

B *Protected sex means sex using a condom*

The safest way to avoid getting an STI is not to have sex at all. The next safest way is to have protected sex with just one partner who has no other sexual partners. If you think you might have contracted an STI, you can ask your GP surgery or genito-urinary medicine (GUM) clinic to give you a simple test.

Sexually transmitted infections (STIs)

Five STIs are discussed below.

HIV

HIV stands for human immunodeficiency virus. This virus is a microorganism that at first causes symptoms that are like those of a cold or flu. These include fever, sore throat and joint pains. Up to 10 years later, the virus attacks a person's immune system, so that they are at increased risk from other bacteria and viruses. A person can have the virus without seeming to be ill. When damage to the immune system does occur, it is called AIDS (acquired immunodeficiency syndrome). Effects on physical health include respiratory infections, such as pneumonia, and digestive disorders, including diarrhoea and cancers.

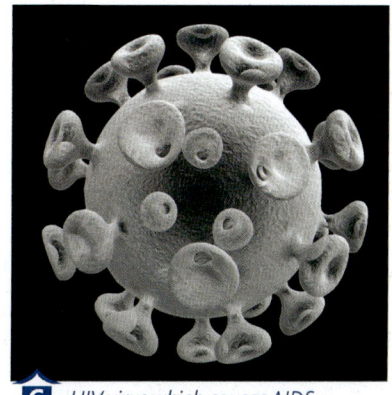

HIV is a very recent disease in humans, and very commonly led to death from AIDS. However, medical science and technology soon developed a treatment that can prevent HIV from developing into AIDS. The treatment includes **antiretroviral drugs**. This treatment can

C *HIV virus which causes AIDS*

enable an infected person to live for a normal lifespan, but it does not cure the infection. Anyone having unprotected sex with the person will be at risk of infection.

Gonorrhoea

Gonorrhoea is caused by bacteria found in semen and vaginal fluid. It most commonly affects men aged 20–24 years and women aged 16–19 years. It is the second most common STI.

The symptoms might not appear until several weeks or months after a person has been infected. An infected person without symptoms can pass on the disease to other people.

Symptoms are slightly different in men and women. About half of women do not have any obvious symptoms. When symptoms are present, they include a discharge from the vagina, pain or discomfort when urinating, and bleeding between periods or heavier periods.

Most men with the infection show symptoms, including discharge from the penis, a need to urinate more often and pain when urinating. The long-term effects for men can include inflammation of the testes. Women can develop pelvic inflammatory disease, which can lead to infertility. Gonorrhoea can be passed from a mother to a baby at birth.

It can be cured with antibiotics.

Chlamydia

Chlamydia is also caused by bacteria. It is now the most common STI. It does not often cause obvious symptoms, and people can be infected for a long time without knowing. In women, it increases the occurrence of cystitis, pelvic pain and discharge from the vagina. If untreated, it can cause pain during intercourse, bleeding between periods and pelvic inflammatory disease, which can lead to infertility.

It can be cured with antibiotics.

D *People can be infected with chlamydia for a long time without knowing*

Herpes

Herpes is caused by the herpes simplex virus. This can cause cold sores around the mouth. It can also affect the genitals. It is then called genital herpes. An infected person might not show any symptoms. In some cases, there are flu-like symptoms and blisters in the genital area. These burst leaving painful sores. In some cases, there is also pain when urinating.

The virus can be controlled with antiviral drugs, which reduce the symptoms but do not cure the infection.

Genital warts

Genital warts are rough raised lumps on the skin that can occur on and around the penis, around and inside the anus and around and inside the vagina. They are caused by the human papilloma virus (**HPV**). Infection with this virus increases the risk of **cervical cancer**.

The symptoms can take weeks or months to appear after a person has been infected. The warts do not usually hurt, but sometimes they itch, become inflamed and bleed. The warts can be reduced or removed by treatments such as creams and surgery. Some people naturally develop immunity to the virus. Although the infection cannot be cured medically, it can be prevented by **immunisation**.

In 2008 an immunisation programme against HPV was started for all adolescent girls in Britain.

> *Study tip*
> Try practice question 5 at the end of this chapter (page 126).

Summary table for revision

E *Sexually transmitted infections*

Infection	Micro-organism(s)	Symptoms	Treatment
HIV	Virus	At first, mild, fever-like symptoms, e.g. sore throat, joint pains After about 10 years, develops into Aids, which damages the immune system and can cause diarrhoea, cancer, pneumonia, and eventually death	No cure for infection Antiretroviral drugs control the infection, preventing Aids and allowing normal lifespan
Gonorrhoea	Bacteria	Symptoms not present at first Then pain when urinating Discharge from penis/vagina Later, pelvic inflammatory disease, possible infertility in women	Antibiotic drugs cure the infection
Chlamydia	Bacteria	Often without symptoms Later, pelvic inflammatory disease, possible infertility in women	Antibiotic drugs cure the infection
Herpes	Virus	Often without symptoms Blisters/sores in genital area	No cure for infection Antiviral drugs reduce symptoms
Genital warts	Virus	Symptoms not present at first Later warts appear Can itch	No cure for infection Immunisation can prevent infection Warts can be removed

6.6 Factors affecting health – genetically inherited diseases

Genetically inherited diseases and health

Objectives
Describe the causes and effects of several genetically inherited diseases.

Meanwhile... in Ramsay MacDonald Street ...

Matt Webster has been told to tidy his room. When baby Danny is a bit older he will sleep in the same room. Naomi offers to help her brother. Matt sulks while Naomi puts piles of Matt's old drawings in a bin-bag. Suddenly she notices something.

'Matt, why have you coloured these trees in red?' Matt glances at the crayon picture, done when he was four years old. 'They look OK to me,' he says. 'Well, they're not,' says Naomi. 'You must be stupid or something. Look, here's a house with a green roof.'

A

A genetically inherited disease is a physical factor that a person cannot control. It is a genetic factor, not a lifestyle factor.

Genetic disorders

The following genetic disorders affect a small number of people.

Down's syndrome

A person with Down's syndrome usually has a characteristic facial appearance, including small features, slanting eyes and a fold on each eyelid. The person is usually short, with stubby hands and feet. Typically the person will have lower than average intelligence, and an affectionate, cheerful personality. Down's syndrome is not actually a genetic disorder and is not inherited in the same way as other disorders described in this section. Instead it is a chromosomal disorder. People with Down's syndrome have an

B A child with Down's syndrome

extra chromosome, i.e. one of their chromosome pairs is actually a set of three. Special education can help children with this syndrome to achieve their potential.

PKU

PKU is short for **phenylketonuria**. This disease, which is also caused by a pair of faulty recessive genes, results in the body being unable to make an enzyme that is important for digesting a chemical found in food. The faulty digestion produces a toxic substance which builds up in the blood stream. This toxin damages body tissues, including the brain. An infant born with PKU is likely to have poor brain development unless the condition is treated. This leads to mental retardation, i.e. low intelligence. For this reason, all newborns are given a simple **screening test** (the heel-prick test). A sample of blood is taken from the heel and tested for PKU. If PKU is found, the person has to keep to a special diet to reduce the production of PKU to safe levels. This diet means the infant should not be fed breast milk, and, for the rest of the person's life, certain foods, including chicken, fish, nuts, cheese and beans, have to be avoided.

Huntington's Disease

Huntington's disease causes of death of nerve cells in the brain. It is a genetic disorder caused by a faulty dominant gene. Only one of these genes (not a pair) is needed for a person to have this disease. It is inherited from a parent (either mother or father) who has the disease. Symptoms usually appear in adulthood, between the ages of around 35 to 45 years. They include forgetfulness, clumsy and jerky movements and personality changes. Eventually the person loses control over their movements, for example finding it difficult to swallow. People with this disease usually live for around 20 years after they have been diagnosed.

> **Study tip**
> The teacher's guide names Down's syndrome, Huntington's disease and Haemophilia as disorders which you might be asked about in an examination. However the other disorders can also be used when giving examples of genetic conditions.

A test for red–green colour blindness; a person without colour blindness will see the word 'COLOUR'

Colour blindness

A person who is colour blind cannot tell the difference between some colours. There are different types of colour blindness, some of which are caused genetically. The commonest genetic form is red–green colour blindness. In this condition, the person cannot tell the difference between something that is coloured red and something coloured green. This means that they have to respond to traffic lights by looking at the position not the colour of the light. This type of colour blindness is caused by a pair of recessive genes on the person's **sex chromosomes**. Females have two X sex chromosomes. A recessive gene on each of the X chromosomes will cause colour blindness. Males have one X and one Y chromosome. The Y chromosome does not have a space for the colour vision gene, so, if a male has one recessive gene on the X chromosome, he will be colour blind.

This does not lead to any other ill-health effects. There is no routine treatment, although some people with colour blindness wear tinted contact lenses that improve their colour vision.

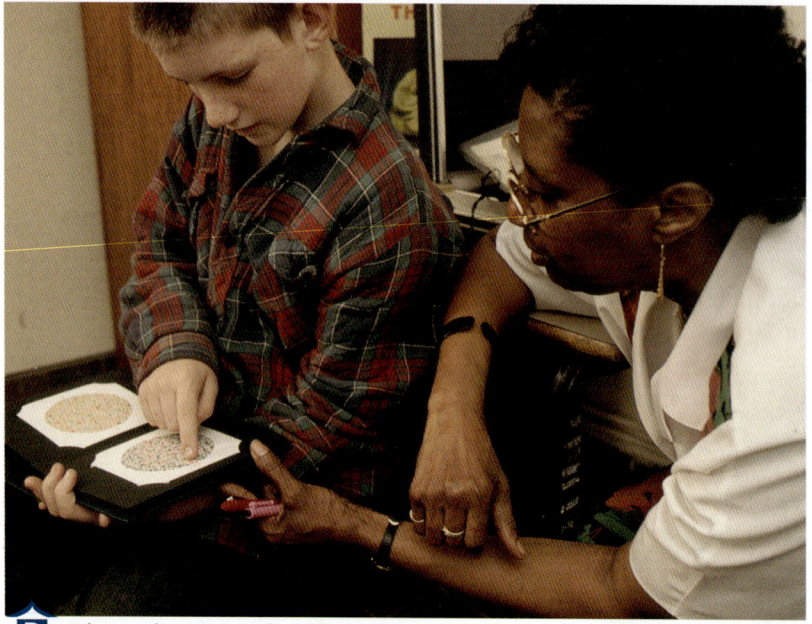

D *A boy undergoing a colour blindness test*

Haemophilia

Haemophilia is a genetic disease in which the person's body cannot make one of the chemicals that help in blood clotting. This chemical is known as a **clotting factor**. Only one faulty gene is needed for haemophilia to occur (not a pair of genes as in PKU). This gene is found on an X chromosome (one of the two sex chromosomes). As males have one X and one Y sex chromosome, haemophilia, although very rare, occurs much more often in males than in females. Males inherit it from the mother only. Mothers of males with haemophilia do not have the condition because they have a healthy gene on their other X chromosome.

The absence of clotting factor means that, when a person with haemophilia has a wound, this takes much longer to stop bleeding than in a normal person. More seriously, internal bleeding is also much more likely, for example into the stomach, brain and joints. Internal bleeding leads to anaemia and can be life threatening.

The disease can be treated by injecting the missing clotting factor into the patient's blood. This is not a cure and has to be repeated, for example when internal bleeding is suspected.

Summary table for revision

D Health effects of genetic disorders

Disorder	Main feature	Cause	Effects on health and wellbeing	Treatment
Down's Syndrome	Facial appearance, Reduced intelligence	One extra chromosome	Reduced school achievement	Special education
Huntington's disease	Nerve (brain) cell death	One faulty dominant gene	Forgetfulness, clumsiness, loss of motor control, personality change	Drugs to reduce symptoms
PKU	Toxin in the blood	Two faulty recessive genes	Damage to organs, e.g. brain	Special diet
Colour blindness	Difficulty in telling colours apart	Two faulty recessive genes in females. One faulty recessive gene in males	Some problems with vision	Tinted lenses
Haemophilia	Failure of blood to clot	One faulty recessive gene in males	Loss of blood, anaemia, internal bleeding	Regular injections of clotting factor

Activities

1. Re-read the description of Matt's drawings (page 100). Think of one reason for Matt's unusual choice of colours.
2. Could any other member of the Webster family also be affected? Look back to the Introduction (page 5).

Study tip

Try practice question 6 at the end of this chapter (page 126).

6.7 Factors affecting health – preventing illness and managing risk

Meanwhile...

... in Ramsay MacDonald Street ...

At the flat above Number 6, Nelson Winters is blowing hard into a tube and writing down a number from the scale on the side. He does this three times, and then he adds a point to a graph he has drawn. It shows a wiggly line with peaks and troughs, but a rising trend. Nelson has had to use his inhaler more often since his family moved to the street.

In the Aziz store, Jenny and Juliet Webster are chatting with Jasmeena. 'I had that smear test once,' says Juliet. 'Never again. There's no way doing that test is going to stop you getting cancer. It stands to reason.' Her daughter Jenny agrees, 'If you're going to get cancer, you're going to get it, and that's all there is to it. They're always trying to make you do something or stop you from doing something else. Why can't they let people live their own lives for heaven's sake?' 'It's like banning smoking,' says Jenny. 'It's interfering in people's private lives.'

'Well, maybe,' says Jasmeena, 'but I always go for my smear test and the breast thingy. I don't mind them taking pictures of my boobs, just so long as they don't print them in the newspaper.'

'But what's it for? What good does it do?' asks Jenny. 'I don't know. I'm not an expert,' replies Jasmeena, 'but I'm not going to turn down medical care when it's free. Lots of other countries you have to pay, you know. Why don't you ask Katya about it?'

'I'm keeping out of her way,' says Jenny, 'otherwise she'll go on at me to let Danny have those jabs.'

A

Objectives

Describe different methods of preventing illness.

Explain how health monitoring is carried out.

Explain the purpose of risk management.

Illness prevention

Illness prevention is a physical factor affecting health and wellbeing. There are several methods of preventing illness, and these contribute positively to health and wellbeing. These are:

- immunisation
- screening
- health monitoring
- safety and risk management
- health promotion.

Immunisation

A person is immune to an infectious disease if their body contains factors that can kill the disease organism. The human body has an **immune system** that fights infections. For example, if a person catches a disease, such as measles, they usually become quite ill. After a while, the person's immune system attacks the infection. If the person gets better, they then have immunity against measles in the future. This is natural immunity. Sometimes, especially with people who have weak immune systems, they die before they can become immune.

To prevent this, a procedure called **vaccination** is used. A vaccine is a weakened form of a disease organism. This is injected into the body. The immune system easily overcomes the weakened organisms and develops immunity. Vaccination has a very low risk and is much safer than letting people catch a disease from which they might die.

Examples of vaccination include:

- **Combined DTP-Polio-Hib vaccination** This protects against several diseases including diphtheria, tetanus, whooping cough, polio, pneumonia and meningitis. It is given in several doses by injection at two, three and four months old, and then again at the ages of around five and 16 years.
- **Combined MMR vaccine** This is used to immunise infants and children against measles, mumps and rubella. Three doses are given by injection when infants are nine, 12 and 15 months old. A booster injection is given a few years later.

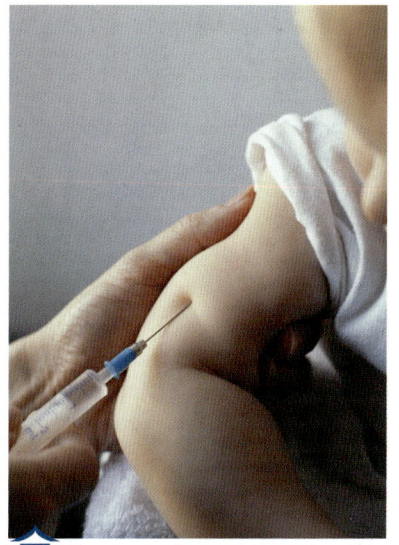

B *Vaccination is much safer than letting infants catch a disease from which they might die*

Screening

Screening is a process in which all the members of an at-risk population are checked to see whether or not they have a disease. Screening takes place before a disease has had a chance to do much damage, and at a stage when it can usually be treated effectively or cured.

Examples of health screening include:

- **The heel-prick test for PKU** All newborns are tested at two weeks old. This is early enough to prevent the brain and tissue damage that would otherwise occur.
- **Breast cancer screening** The population most at risk from breast cancer is women aged 50 to 70 years. They are invited for screening. An X-ray image of the breasts is taken. This is called a **mammogram**. It is checked for signs of breast cancer, which can be treated successfully if it is caught early. Women are invited for screening every three years.
- **Cervical cancer screening** Adult women are screened using the **smear test**. This takes a sample of tissue from the neck of the womb (the cervix), using a spatula or small brush. Women are screened from around 20 to 64 years old (the age varies in different parts of the UK). This screening test is repeated every three to five years.

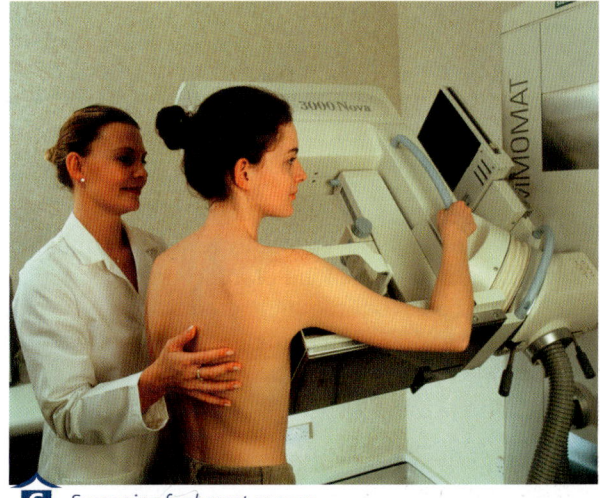

C *Screening for breast cancer*

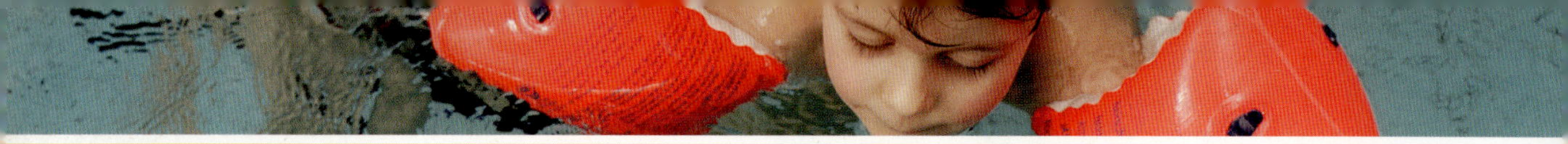

Health monitoring

Health monitoring means checking a person's health regularly. It is not the same as screening because there is no particular target population.

Health monitoring is important in people who are already ill, are at risk of becoming ill or are recovering from illness. GPs often monitor the health of patients who visit them, for example by checking their blood pressure. Hospital patients are also regularly monitored.

Examples of health monitoring include:

- getting children with asthma to check their **peak flow** regularly, to measure how well the respiratory system is working
- checking a person's blood pressure to see whether they have hypertension. Hypertension is a risk factor for strokes, diabetes and heart disease. Treating hypertension can reduce the risks of developing these diseases. Monitoring blood pressure is important during pregnancy and in older people
- **blood testing** – a small sample of blood is taken and sent to a laboratory for testing. One test is to measure the amount of blood sugar present. A high level can mean that the person has diabetes. This can then be treated. Monitoring for diabetes is important in older people who are most at risk.

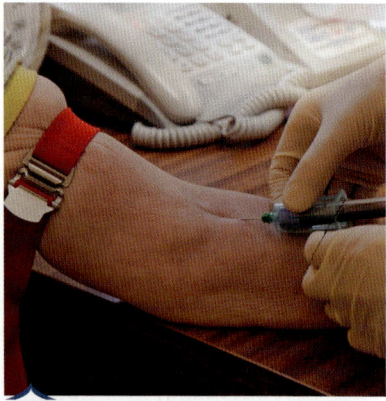

D *Diabetes is diagnosed by a blood test*

Methods of monitoring health

Health monitoring involves measuring several indicators of physical health. These include:

- taking a person's temperature
- measuring a person's pulse rate
- measuring blood pressure
- measuring the peak flow of air out of the lungs
- measuring the level of sugars in a person's blood
- weighing a person
- measuring a person's height
- calculating a person's **body mass index** (BMI), using their weight and height.

Body temperature

The normal human body temperature is around 37 °C. If a person's temperature is around 5°C lower than this, they have **hypothermia** and need to be warmed up. Hypothermia is a condition, in which a person becomes confused, loses consciousness and can die.

If a person's temperature is around 1°C or 2°C warmer than normal they have a fever. Fever is usually a sign that the body's immune system is fighting some kind of infection. The high temperature helps this process, but too high a temperature is very dangerous. A temperature of 38 °C is regarded as a fever in children. Normal body temperature is the same for people in all life stages. Temperature can be measured using a thermometer.

Blood pressure

Blood pressure is usually measured while a person is relaxed and at rest. Blood pressure rises and falls with each heartbeat. For this reason, blood pressure meters give two readings. The high reading is called **systolic blood pressure**. This is the high pressure that results at the moment the heart pumps out a pulse of blood. The low reading is called **diastolic blood pressure**. This is the pressure between pulses. Because pressure varies with body position, blood pressure is measured with the patient sitting down and with the arm resting on a table.

Blood pressure can be measured using a **sphygmomanometer**. This has an inflatable cuff that is wrapped around a seated person's upper arm. The cuff is inflated with air and grips so tightly that it temporarily stops blood flowing in the arm. The air pressure inside the cuff is measured by a glass tube with a column of mercury inside. To find systolic blood pressure, you gradually let air out of the cuff until the air pressure is low enough to allow a pulse to flow through the arm. You listen to the pulse using a stethoscope on the arm just below the cuff. The pressure is read off in millimetres of mercury (mmHg). To find diastolic pressure, more air is let out of the cuff until there is no sound of a pulse on the arm. This means that the cuff is not restricting blood flow, so the pressure inside the cuff is the same as that inside the body at the moment of lowest pressure, between pulses.

Other types of blood pressure meter also use a cuff on the upper arm but are easier to use. They usually have a microphone and speaker to amplify the sound of the pulse. Some electronic blood pressure monitors can be worn on the wrist, although these are not usually as accurate as upper-arm models.

The average systolic blood pressure is 120 mmHg, and the average diastolic pressure is 80 mmHg. This is usually written as 120/80 ('a hundred and twenty over eighty'). Blood pressures at birth are lower – around 80/50. Normal blood pressure rises as a person gets older. A young, fit adult might have a blood pressure of 110/70. A person with a blood pressure of around 140/90 or more has high blood pressure (hypertension).

During activity, blood pressure naturally rises. It falls again when activity stops. A person's blood pressure will typically vary by around 30 to 40 mmHg in a day.

Pulse rate

Every time the heart pumps out blood there is a brief increase in pressure. This is called a pulse. The pulse can be felt wherever an artery is near the surface of the skin. You can measure a person's pulse rate by placing the second and third fingers of one hand on the skin above the artery in the person's wrist or at the side of the neck and counting the number of pulses in a minute. To get a rough figure, you can count pulses for 30 seconds and double the number.

The normal pulse rate for a healthy adult at rest is between 60 and 80 beats per minute. Within this range, girls over 12 and women usually have higher pulse rates than men and boys. Children and older people usually have higher normal pulse rates.

It is usual to measure pulse rate when a person is at rest. This is called the **resting pulse rate**.

People who are very fit tend to have lower (slower) than normal pulse rates because their bodies work so efficiently. A person whose resting pulse rate is higher than normal for their age and sex is likely to be unfit and might have heart disease. The pulse is high because the heart has to pump quickly just to keep the body going, even at rest.

Another way of using pulse rate to measure health is to get the person to take part in some exercise. The best way to do this is to have the same standard exercise, so that different people can be compared. One type of exercise is to run on a gym treadmill, set at a fixed speed for a fixed amount of time. This is called a **stress test**. It is a test that puts a slight stress on a person's cardiac and respiratory systems; it has nothing to do with the stress that results from **stressors** (stressful experiences).

Pulse rate during exercise will be higher than pulse rate at rest. This is because the heart has to pump blood faster to keep up with the body's demand for oxygen and food. The fittest person will show the least increase in pulse rate. The least fit person will show the greatest increase in pulse rate.

Another measure that can be used is **recovery pulse rate**. This is a person's pulse rate one minute after exercise has stopped. A third useful measure is **recovery time**. This is the time taken, after exercise has stopped, for the pulse rate to return to the resting pulse rate level.

Peak flow

Peak flow is a measure of how well the respiratory system is working. Peak flow means the maximum rate at which a person can blow air out of their lungs. A person whose respiratory system is working well will have a higher peak flow rate than a person who has respiratory problems, such as asthma or bronchitis. Peak flow is measured using a **peak flow meter**. This can be a simple arrangement made out of cardboard. The meter is first set to zero. Then the person takes a deep breath and blows into the meter as fast and as hard as they can. The meter gives a reading in litres per minute. It is usual to do this three times. The highest score is taken as the person's peak flow. People with asthma are usually given a simple peak flow meter so that they can check their health regularly. More accurate meters have a flexible tube leading into an electronic device with a digital display.

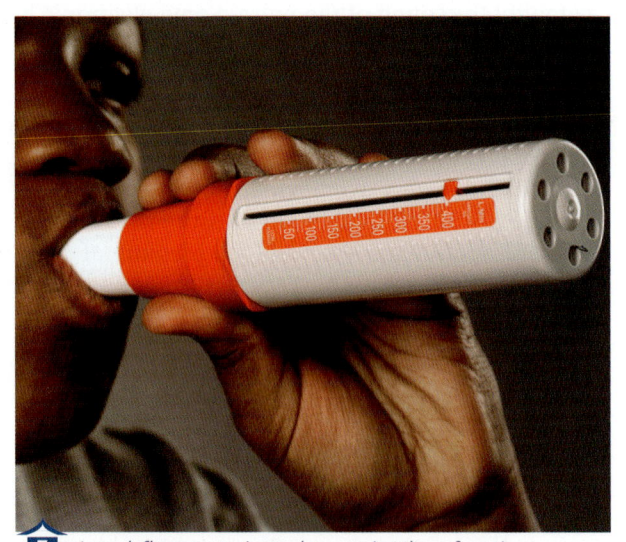

E *A peak flow meter is used to monitor lung function*

Peak flow is highest in young adult men, at an average of around 630 decimetres cubed (dm³) per minute. Women usually have a lower rate of around 470 dm³ per minute at age 30. Children have a much lower peak flow rate. In later adulthood, peak flow is also reduced.

Note that people working in health care use the units 'litres per minute'. For the purpose of the assessment you should use dm³ per minute.

Blood sugar testing

The blood contains sugars that are used by body cells to produce energy. A test of blood sugar can indicate whether or not a person has diabetes. Usually, a small sample of blood is taken and sent to a laboratory for analysis. Small electronic blood sugar monitors are available that will give an instant result on a drop of blood taken by pricking a finger.

Body mass index (BMI)

Body mass index is not itself a measurement. It can be worked out after measuring a person's weight in kilograms and height in metres. A person's BMI is their weight in kilograms divided by the square of their height in metres. For example, a person who is 2 metres tall would divide their weight by 2 squared, i.e. 4.

A person who weighs 80 kg and is 2 metres tall would have a BMI of

$$\frac{80}{4} = 20 \, kg/m^2$$

A tall thin person will have a lower BMI than a shorter thin person. Both of them would have lower BMIs than a short fat person. A normal BMI is in the range between 18.5 and 25 kg/m². A BMI higher than 30 kg/m² indicates that the person is probably obese.

Note that BMI is often given justs as a number – without the units. For example, a BMI of 25 kg/m² is simple expressed as a BMI of 25.

BMI can indicate health because it shows whether a person is in the normal range or not. A person who is underweight might be ill, and a person who is overweight or obese is at greater risk of illness.

Safety and risk management

Risk management is another physical factor that can positively affect health and wellbeing.

Risk management means reducing danger to workers and members of the public. Organisations have to work out the risks involved in everything they do and balance these against the benefits that might result.

Schools and workplaces have to carry out **risk assessments**. A risk assessment includes identifying the hazards that are present, who might be harmed and how, how much risk is present and what precautions can be taken to reduce it. Risk management does not aim to remove all risk. Instead, the aim is to enable the maximum benefit for the minimum risk.

For example, a school organises a skiing trip for pupils. The benefits of the trip might include helping pupils to be more independent, using a foreign language and developing their fitness and motor skills. The risks are those involved with travel and in moving fast on snow slopes. The best way to reduce the risk is not to go on the trip, but this would not benefit the children. Risk management enables the benefits to be achieved, while keeping the risks small.

These are some health and wellbeing effects of risk management:

- **Physical** Risk management enables people to take part in activities that might improve health, while taking precautions to reduce physical injury or harm.
- **Intellectual** Risk management helps people to think more deeply about what they want to achieve. It increases knowledge and awareness about unexpected events.
- **Emotional** Risk management enables people to feel safe and yet do things that might be exciting or adventurous.
- **Social** Risk management usually requires people to work together and to protect each other.

links

You can find BMI calculators on the internet, for example at
www.eatwell.gov.uk/healthydiet/healthyweight/bmicalculator

F *Risk management aims to give maximum benefit for minimum risk*

Health promotion

Health promotion means educating people about risks to health and about how to have a healthy lifestyle. It aims to improve health by discouraging people from risky behaviour. It includes education in school about diet, health, exercise, sex and substance abuse. It also includes publicity campaigns using posters, websites and TV advertisements. An example is a TV campaign to discourage people from driving after drinking alcohol.

G Health promotion campaign

Compared with some other methods of illness prevention, health promotion does not seem to be very effective. There are several reasons for this:

- People who have risky lifestyles might ignore health promotion messages because they make them feel anxious or guilty.
- People might not believe the information given. Instead, they might rely on what friends or relatives say.
- Some people feel that health promotion messages are a form of interference with their freedom to do as they wish.

Many people are aware of the content of health promotion messages but do not act on these messages. Hospital nurses know a lot about healthy lifestyles, but are they all slim non-smokers?

In contrast, legislation and taxation are much more effective. For example, the recent legislation making smoking in pubs and restaurants illegal has led to many people giving up smoking. Tax increases on alcohol and tobacco can also lead to a reduction in consumption.

Preventing illness and managing risk at different life stages

Infancy

- At two weeks, all infants in the UK have the heel-prick test for PKU.
- At two, three and four months, the DTP-Polio-Hib vaccine is given.
- Three doses of the MMR vaccine are given, normally at 9, 12 and 15 months.
- Infant development is monitored by health visitors.

Childhood

- Between three and five years old, children get a booster MMR vaccination.
- At around five years, a booster injection is given for DTP-Polio-Hib.
- Children with asthma are asked to monitor their own health using a peak flow meter.
- Schools have to assess and manage risks at school and in out-of-school activities.

H Infant development is monitored by health visitors

Adolescence

- Between 12 and 13 years old, girls are vaccinated against the sexually transmitted infection HPV.
- At around 16 years old, a booster injection is given for DTP-Polio-Hib.
- Schools, sports clubs and youth clubs have to assess and manage risks.
- Adolescents receive education about lifestyle and health.

Adulthood

- Women are screened for cervical cancer. Women over 50 are screened for breast cancer.
- Pregnant women have their blood pressure checked.
- People who visit the GP or have some medical treatment will have their blood pressure checked and might have blood tests.
- People travelling to some countries on holiday or for work should be vaccinated against some diseases that occur there; for example, travellers to Africa or Asia should be vaccinated against diphtheria.
- Workplaces have to assess and manage risks for their employees.

Later adulthood

A screening programme for bowel cancer is being introduced for people aged 60 to 69 years. This will screen people every two years.

Some health centres and GP practices offer older people regular health checks. People who visit the GP or have some medical treatment will have their blood pressure checked and may have blood tests. Older people are also offered vaccination against flu every autumn.

Organisations providing services for older people (e.g. residential homes) have to assess and manage risks, so as to provide services safely without reducing the quality of life.

> **Activity**
>
> 1. Re-read the description of the neighbours (page 104).
>   a. Give two screening methods that were mentioned in Jasmeena's shop.
>   b. The three women don't understand how screening prevents illness. What explanation could you give them?
>   c. What's wrong with Nelson?
>   d. Pick out two other methods of illness prevention that were mentioned in the description.
>
> **Study tip**
>
> Try practice questions 7 and 8 at the end of this chapter (page 127).

Summary table for revision

1 *Preventing illness and managing risk*

Method	How it works	Example
Vaccination	Inject weakened disease organisms Body develops immunity	DTP-Polio-Hib MMR (measles, mumps and rubella vaccines)
Health screening	Check all members of target at-risk population Treat those who show the disease	Heel-prick test for PKU Mammogram for breast cancer Smear test for cervical cancer Bowel cancer screening
Health monitoring	Routinely check people when they visit the GP or receive treatment Treat as necessary	Peak flow metering for asthma patients Measuring blood pressure Blood testing for diabetes
Risk management	Carry out risk assessment Reduce risk but balance it against benefits	Reducing risk but keeping productivity high in a factory Reducing risk but providing challenge and enjoyment on a school trip
Health promotion	Enables people to learn how to stay healthy and avoid illness	Sex education Substance abuse education 'Don't drink and drive' campaigns

6.8 Factors affecting health – lack of personal hygiene

Lack of personal hygiene and health

Lack of **personal hygiene** is another physical factor that can negatively influence health and wellbeing. It is also a lifestyle factor over which people can have control. Keeping the body clean is called personal hygiene. It includes washing the skin and hair and cleaning the teeth and fingernails. An important reason for personal hygiene is to be attractive to other people or, at least, not repulsive.

Personal hygiene can also reduce the risk of spreading infections. One important precaution is to wash hands thoroughly after going to the toilet and before preparing food. As well as removing dirt, washing removes oils that are produced by the skin. It also removes some of the micro-organisms such as bacteria that live on the skin and can produce some **body odours**. Bacteria on armpit hair can produce a strong body odour.

There are some health risks from poor personal hygiene. There is some risk of infection if, for example, microorganisms in excrement enter the blood stream through a cut on the skin. Poor dental hygiene increases the risk of tooth decay.

> **Objectives**
> Explain the problems that might result from lack of personal hygiene.

A Washing hands is part of personal hygiene

Meanwhile... ... in Ramsay MacDonald Street ...

Katya is going to give her four-year-old daughter a bath. Magda does not like having a bath. Even before the taps are turned on she starts screaming at her mother. Katya knows how to deal with Magda's tantrums. She knows that getting angry with Magda will only make it harder for the little girl to control her emotions. She knows that hitting infants and children is wrong and not effective. So she says, 'I'll just go and change the sheets on your bed. I won't be long.' On her own in the bathroom, Magda sits on the floor and looks at the pattern on the bathmat. She completely forgets her anger. Twenty minutes later, Magda has had her bath and Katya is drying her. Magda asks, 'But Mum, why do I have to have baths?' Katya replies, 'Well, if you didn't have a bath you might stink of sweat and wee and poo. People wouldn't like to come near you. They might not want to be friends. You don't want to stink do you?' Magda asks, 'Do you and Daddy have to have baths?' Katya says, 'Daddy and me have showers. It's quicker.' 'Is that why you don't stink?' asks Magda. 'Yes. We also put on deodorant, like this.' Katya mimes the process and gets out a stick of deodorant for Magda to look at.

Magda sniffs it and says, 'That will make you stink of the odorant.'

Health and wellbeing effects of lack of personal hygiene include:

- **Physical** Poor personal hygiene can lead to some risk of infection.
- **Intellectual** There are no direct effects.
- **Emotional** A person with poor personal hygiene is likely to lack confidence among other people and to have low self-esteem.

- **Social** A person with poor personal hygiene might become socially isolated. Other people might be repelled by the person's smell and appearance.

Personal hygiene for care workers

Clients in health and social care often have weak immune systems. They are more likely to become ill with infections. The clients at greater risk include infants, people who are already ill and older people.

Personal hygiene is important for care workers in places like crèches, hospital wards and residential homes for older people. Care workers in this situation should wash their hands properly and make sure that their clients are kept clean too.

Hygiene in different life stages

Infancy

Hygiene is of particular importance in infancy because of **incontinence**; young infants cannot control excretion; they have to wear nappies, which must be changed frequently. During a nappy change, the infant is usually washed as well.

Infants are often kept away from dirt. This can help to reduce the risk of infections, but it can have a negative effect too. Exposure to dirt and infection during infancy can act to stimulate the immune system that will protect the person from infections throughout their lives. There is some evidence that infants who are kept very clean and free from dirt are more likely to develop allergies as they grow up.

C *Babies wear nappies which need changing regularly*

Childhood

It is easier to maintain hygiene in children, because they are able to use the toilet themselves. Children usually only have poor hygiene if they are neglected by their parents. For example, some children are not bathed very often and their clothes are not washed often enough.

Adolescence

The development of armpit hair at puberty leads to an increased chance of body odour. At the same time, many adolescents become interested in being physically attractive. As a result, hygiene practices become more important at this stage.

Adulthood

The personal hygiene practices established during adolescence are usually continued during adulthood.

Later adulthood

For some older people hygiene routines can become more difficult to perform. For example, a person with limited mobility and flexibility might find it hard to take a bath or shower. Older people with memory loss can simply forget to wash themselves or their clothes. Some older people become incontinent, and this greatly increases the difficulties of keeping clean and smelling nice.

> **Study tip**
> - Try practice question 9 at the end of this chapter (page 127).
> - Remember that the factors affecting health and wellbeing that have been described so far are all physical factors. Economic, social and environmental factors are also important. These are described in Sections 6.9 to 6.11, through pages 114–125.

6.9 Factors affecting health – economic factors

Economic factors and health

Economic factors include financial resources, poverty, work and unemployment. People might not be able to control these factors.

Adequate financial resources

Adequate financial resources means having enough money to pay for housing, food, utility bills (gas, water and electricity), clothing, transport and leisure activities. Adequate financial resources can help people to stay healthy for several reasons. It means that people can afford:

- to pay for food, so they have enough to eat
- a variety of foods, so they have a balanced diet
- to cook food and maintain food hygiene (e.g. by washing plates in hot water)
- housing that is safe, easy to clean, not damp or infested with vermin
- leisure activities to provide exercise and promote wellbeing.

Poverty

Poverty is a situation in which a person does not have adequate financial resources. In theory, no-one in Britain should be in poverty, because of the system of cash benefits designed to prevent poverty.

In practice, some people do experience poverty. For example, some illegal immigrants and legal migrant workers are paid illegally low wages (below the national minimum wage). Another example is of people cheated out of their money by relatives. This includes children neglected by their parents and older people cheated by their children.

Links between poverty and health

People in poverty often have much worse health than people with adequate financial resources. For example, infants in poor families are more likely to die than infants in more well-off families. Death in infancy is called **infant mortality**. In addition, babies born to poorer families tend to have lower than average birth weights.

Poorer people are likely to have a shorter life expectancy than wealthy people. A larger proportion of poor people die from lung cancer, are obese and die after a first heart attack compared with the rest of the population.

> **Objectives**
> Explain the benefits of adequate financial resources and stimulating work.
>
> Explain the problems that might result from poverty and unemployment.

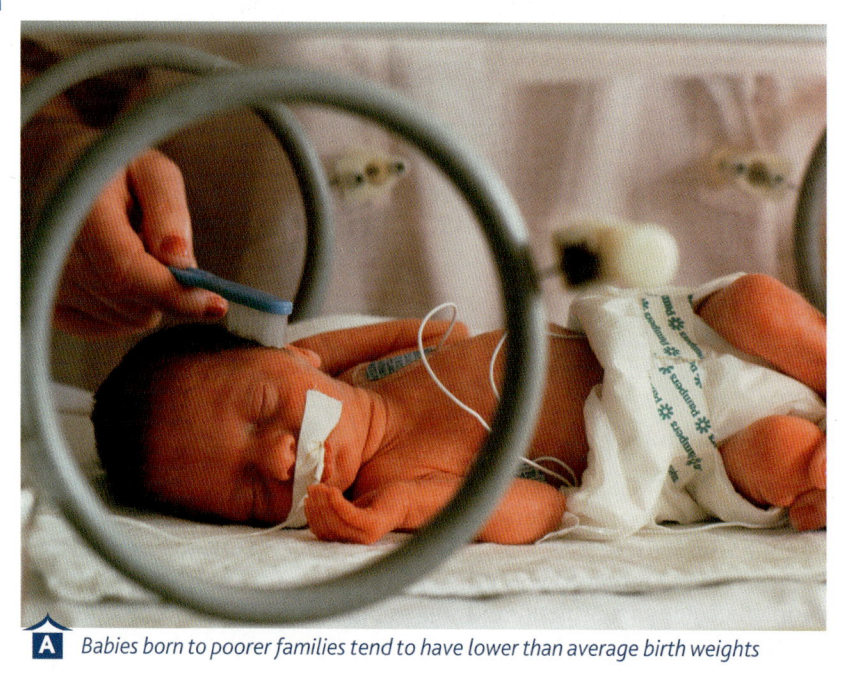

A Babies born to poorer families tend to have lower than average birth weights

Does poverty cause ill-health?

People who are so poor that they cannot afford enough food are likely to become ill. This level of poverty is rare in Britain. Surprisingly, in Britain, poor people are more likely to become ill as a result of eating too much.

People who cannot afford good-quality housing are likely to be less healthy. For example, people living in a damp caravan with no hot water and no working toilet. Poverty can also cause continued ill health for people who cannot afford to pay for health services. This mainly applies in countries where health services have to be paid for but not in Britain, where the services are mostly free.

In many cases in Britain, poverty is not the direct cause of ill health. Instead, poverty and ill health are linked in different ways. People who already have poor health might be too ill to work, so they will have less income than those who work. People who have very low educational achievement are more likely not to know about balanced diets or health risks. This increases the chances that they will have risky behaviour, such as smoking and drinking alcohol while pregnant. At the same time, their low educational achievement makes it unlikely that they will earn much money. They might not know about some health services, or they might not be able to read letters asking them to attend health screening. They might not be very good at managing what money they have: for example, they might spend too much on wants and not enough on needs.

Poverty and lifestyle

Poorer people tend to have less healthy lifestyles than better-off people. For example, poorer people are more likely to smoke. This is one reason why a larger proportion of poor people die from lung cancer. Also, poorer people tend to have diets higher in carbohydrates and fats. This partly explains why a larger proportion of poor people are obese, and why more die after a first heart attack. Poorer people also tend to have lower birth weight and more premature babies. This partly results from a tendency to smoke and drink alcohol while pregnant.

These are some of the negative effects of poverty on health and wellbeing:

- **Physical** There is likely to be little variety in diet and lack of access to exercise (e.g. because poorer people are unable to pay for gym membership).
- **Intellectual** School education is free in Britain. However, poor children might be unable to afford educational aids for use at home, such as computers.
- **Emotional** Worries about money can cause stress and anxiety. Not having as much money as other people can lead to low self-esteem.
- **Social** A very poor person might not be able to afford to go out with friends to pubs, clubs or restaurants.

Work

On balance, work is very good for a person's health. This is most true of stimulating work, i.e. work that is interesting and challenging. Work that is boring or stressful is not so good for health.

These are some of the positive effects of work on health and wellbeing:

- **Physical** Most work requires some physical activity, which helps to maintain fitness. Working with other people requires a person to have a good standard of hygiene.
- **Intellectual** Some jobs are stimulating; they require people to think and solve problems.
- **Emotional** A person's work can be an important part of their self-concept. Doing a worthwhile job or doing your job well can increase self-esteem.
- **Social** Most jobs involve some social contact, such as with customers and work colleagues, so work increases a person's social circle.

Unemployment

A person is unemployed when they are eligible to work but do not have a job. Long-term unemployment is a major problem. A person who is unemployed for months or years can lose some of the habits and skills of work. This can make it even harder for them to get a job. Long-term unemployment is more likely among people who have few job skills and low educational achievement.

B *People enjoy stimulating and rewarding work*

These are some of the negative effects of unemployment on health and wellbeing:

- **Physical** An unemployed person might be less active or less motivated to maintain personal hygiene.
- **Intellectual** Unemployment is unstimulating, and boredom can be a problem.
- **Emotional** Unemployment can lower self-esteem. Unemployed people might think of themselves as useless. Lack of activity and lack of pressure can be depressing.
- **Social** Unemployment can increase social isolation.

Life stages, work and unemployment

Most people who work are in the adult life stage. Towards the end of this stage, or at the start of the later adulthood stage, it is usual for people to retire from work. Many people are pleased to retire, but for some of these the reality is less enjoyable than they expected. This is partly because of the loss of social contact and partly because of the loss to a person's self-concept.

Study tip
Try practice question 10 at the end of this chapter (page 127).

Chapter 6   The nature of health and wellbeing   117

6.10 Factors affecting health – social factors

Social factors and health

Social factors affecting heath include education, leisure activity, relationships, social isolation and stress.

> **Objectives**
>
> Describe the positive benefits of education, leisure and supportive relationships.
>
> Explain the problems that might result from social isolation and stress.

Education

Education is a factor that people are not always able to control. A child might not have a choice of what subjects they study. However, children and adolescents do have some control over how much effort they put into their own education.

These are some of the positive effects of education on a person's health and wellbeing:

- **Physical** Education enables people to learn about ways to stay healthy and improve their health. Pupils and students can learn about a balanced diet, the importance of physical activity and how to avoid disease. School education usually includes some physical activity too.
- **Intellectual** Education can be stimulating for people who believe it will benefit them. People with a negative attitude to education are likely to be bored by it.
- **Emotional** Education can improve a person's self-esteem and sense of achievement. Finding out that you are good at something can contribute to self-concept. Some teachers provide emotional support for pupils and students who are having problems.
- **Social** Education brings people into contact with a large number of peers.

A *There are social benefits to going to school*

Leisure activity

Leisure is the time people have available when they are not at work or asleep. For many people it includes evenings, weekends and holidays. How people use their leisure is a lifestyle factor, over which people have quite a lot of control.

These are some of the positive effects of leisure on a person's health and wellbeing:

- **Physical** It provides time in which people can take exercise, which improves health and wellbeing.
- **Intellectual** It enables people to follow interests that make intellectual demands. For example, people can use leisure time to research their family history, to take part in pub quizzes and to read books.

B *Leisure provides time in which people can take exercise*

- **Emotional** Leisure provides a break from the stresses and pressures of work, enabling the person to feel more calm and relaxed.
- **Social** Leisure gives people opportunities to spend time with family members and friends.

Supportive relationships

Some relationships are difficult for people to have control over. For example, children cannot choose their parents. However, children, adolescents and adults can choose their friends. A person's relationships do not usually have a direct effect on physical health, although relationships have a big influence on wellbeing.

Supportive relationships can contribute indirectly to physical health. People in close relationships tend to look after and protect each other, providing safety: for example, parents getting access to health care for their children.

Supportive relationships can increase wellbeing in several ways.

- Physical contact, such as cuddling, is pleasurable for most people of any age.
- Self-esteem is increased by knowing that other people like you.
- Being with other people can be interesting and stimulating.
- Relationships give people a feeling of security.

Relationship effects in different life stages

Infancy

A relationship with a parent or parent is very important for the wellbeing of an infant. Parents feed the infant, keep the infant clean and protect the infant. Parents also provide play opportunities that aid development. Once an infant attaches, the presence of the parent provides a feeling of safety.

Infants who are neglected by their parents are more at risk from disease and injury. A neglecting parent might not feed or wash the infant properly. A neglecting parent might not take the infant to the GP for immunisations or for medical treatment.

Childhood

A relationship with parents is important for the same reasons in childhood as in infancy. In addition, a child's self-esteem is affected by attention and approval from parents and friends (peers). If parents have a troubled relationship, this can reduce a child's self-esteem and feeling of safety.

C Children benefit from support from their parents

Adolescence

Adolescents tend to rely on parents for food, shelter, clean clothes and protection. Relationships with peers become more important for emotional wellbeing. Unlike parents, peers do not have a responsibility for protecting adolescents from harm. As a result, some adolescents encourage others into risky behaviour. This risky behaviour includes substance misuse and unprotected sex.

Adolescents who have a strong romantic relationship (with a girlfriend or boyfriend) are more likely to be protective of each other.

Adulthood

Adults who have long-lasting romantic relationships, and who are employed, have plenty of opportunities for social support. These relationships can also contribute to a person's self-esteem.

Romantic relationships in which one or both partners become discontented can lead to anxiety, depression, stress and loss of self-esteem. For example, the process of getting a divorce can be very stressful.

Adults who are not in a romantic relationship and are unemployed can become socially isolated and have less support.

D *People in close relationships tend to look after and protect each other*

Later adulthood

In later adulthood, people tend to have fewer relationships and can become socially isolated. The death of a husband, wife or partner is one reason. Some older people lose mobility and are less able to meet other people as a result. Other family members, especially grown-up children, can provide some support and protection. For example, an adult daughter might drive her mother to hospital for an appointment.

Social isolation

A person who has few or no regular contacts with other people is socially isolated. The isolated person has very little **social interaction**. Some people choose to be socially isolated and prefer this to having family relationships and friendships. Most people who are socially isolated would prefer more contact with others. This is a factor that people usually do not have much control over.

People with severe mental disorders are likely to become socially isolated. This can result in hospitalisation or imprisonment, which also reduces contact with other family members. Social isolation is also quite likely among older people, partly because of the death of a spouse and partly because of a loss of mobility. Negative effects of social isolation on health and wellbeing include:

- a lack of support from others
- a lack of protection
- a decline in hygiene, diet and self-care
- loneliness.

E *People with mental disorders are likely to be socially isolated*

Stress

Stress is a person's response to events or thoughts that are difficult or challenging. It is a response to stressors. A typical stressor is a work situation in which a person has to carry out a difficult task in a limited time. Here are two examples:

- In telesales work, an employee telephones people to try to sell them some goods or services. The telesales person has a limited time to get the other person's interest and also has to achieve a certain number of sales to satisfy the employer. During the work, the salesperson is likely to be verbally abused by some of the possible customers.
- A junior hospital doctor is working in the Accident and Emergency department of a hospital on a Saturday night. A large number of casualties arrive, some of them severely injured and some of them drunk. The doctor has to treat patients quickly, to improve their chances of recovery. At the same time, she might be at risk of violence from some of the patients.

F *Stress can occur in difficult and challenging job roles*

Some people exposed to stressors like these will suffer from stress. Others will not. It depends on personality and experience. Some people experience stress as a result of situations that are very mild stressors, such as being late for a train. Others can remain calm in life-threatening situations. People do not usually have much control over this factor.

Stress can have negative effects on health and wellbeing in the following ways:

- **Physical** Stress can raise blood pressure in the long term. It can also lead to disturbed sleep, tiredness, headaches and loss of appetite.
- **Intellectual** Stress can reduce a person's ability to concentrate.
- **Emotional** Stress can lead to irritability, anxiety and depression.
- **Social** Stress can put a strain on relationships and make a person less able to treat others well.

> **Study tip**
> Try practice question 11 at the end of this chapter (page 127).

6.11 Factors affecting health – environmental factors

Housing

Housing is inadequate if it:

- is dirty and untidy
- is damp (e.g. lets rainwater in)
- has an unsafe power supply (e.g. electrical wiring in poor condition or gas leaks)
- has poor ventilation (e.g. windows that do not open)
- has no heating or is draughty
- has no hot or cold water
- has too little space for the number of people living there
- has damaged bathroom and sanitary fittings
- lacks comfortable beds
- is infested by vermin
- is not fitted with safety equipment (e.g. smoke alarms).

The problem with a house being dirty, damp or infested with vermin is that these can increase the risk of infections. Damp helps the growth of moulds, which produce spores that can cause respiratory problems. Lack of heating can lead to a person's body temperature dropping dangerously low, causing hypothermia.

Houses that are untidy, poorly maintained and without safety equipment increase the risk of accidents. For example, objects left on stairs or in doorways increase the risk of falls. Poor wiring can lead to a risk of electrocution. Gas leaks are likely to lead to fires or explosions. Lack of safety equipment can mean that people are less likely to escape in the event of a fire breaking out.

> **Objectives**
> Describe the problems that might result from inadequate housing and environmental pollution.

A *Untidy homes can be dangerous*

A house is poorly ventilated if the windows do not open and chimneys or vents are blocked. This can lead to a build-up of poisonous carbon monoxide gas from gas cookers and fires. A lack of washing facilities (e.g. no hot water, no bath or shower) can make it difficult for people to maintain good personal hygiene.

People who live in inadequate housing usually do so because they cannot afford better accommodation, or because they cannot afford to repair their home. This means that they do not have much control over this factor.

These are some of the negative effects of inadequate housing on health and wellbeing:

- **Physical** There is risk of electrocution, fires, carbon monoxide poisoning, infections, allergies and falls.
- **Intellectual** There is not enough space for children to study quietly or to play.
- **Emotional** There is lack of privacy; stress may be caused by uncomfortable living conditions, and these may contribute to low self-esteem.
- **Social** People might not want to invite friends to spend time with them, because of the overcrowded conditions.

Environmental pollution

Environmental pollution includes:

- poor air quality (e.g. air containing smoke particles from vehicles)
- water pollution (e.g. harmful microorganisms or toxic chemicals in drinking water)
- noise pollution (e.g. noise of traffic or loud music)
- radioactivity (e.g. from granite rocks)
- vermin (e.g. rats, fleas and cockroaches).

Although Britain has a very high population density, environmental pollution is low. Water pollution and radioactivity are at very low levels indeed. Tap water in Britain is of excellent quality, so that it is not necessary to buy bottled water.

The main source of radioactivity is in rocks. Granite in particular releases a radioactive gas called radon, which seeps upwards into houses. Nuclear power stations also produce radioactivity but usually at a lower level than that which occurs naturally. Radioactivity slightly increases the risk of cancer.

Air quality in Britain is good except near busy roads, especially in large towns. Poor air quality can make respiratory diseases worse. Smoke particles increase the risk of some cancers, including lung cancer.

Noise pollution is also a problem in built-up areas. This is partly as a result of noise from traffic (e.g. trucks and planes) but also a result of leisure activities, such as music concerts and firework displays. Noise pollution can be harmful to health because it interferes with sleep. It can also be a stressor, leading to anxiety and depression.

B *Smoke pollution can make diseases such as bronchitis worse*

Vermin are most often found where there is a supply of food for them. Food scraps left on the floor in restaurant kitchens, or in plastic bags in the street, are easily found by rats, mice and cockroaches and enable these to breed. One risk to physical health is that excrement from the vermin contaminates food that will be eaten by people. Vermin also reduce wellbeing because they are a source of anxiety for people.

People often have little direct control over environmental pollution. They can contact their local Environmental Health Department, which is responsible for controlling pollution.

These are some of the negative effects of environmental pollution on health and wellbeing:

- **Physical** Lack of sleep, because of noise, and respiratory illness, because of air pollution, are more likely, as is risk of disease spread by vermin.
- **Intellectual** Worry and lack of sleep can reduce concentration.
- **Emotional** Noise and vermin can cause anxiety, irritability and stress.
- **Social** Disputes with noisy neighbours can lead to reduced social contact.

C *Food scraps attract vermin*

Meanwhile... ... in Ramsay MacDonald Street ...

Gail Winters is filling in an application form for a job. Since she and her children arrived in Ramsay MacDonald Street, she has applied for 15 jobs but has had only two interviews. She is very worried about money and also about her children. Shelley has started wetting the bed again, and Nelson's asthma has been worse recently. Part of the problem is the flat they are living in. There are only three rooms. Shelley sleeps in the same room as Gail. Nelson sleeps on the settee. The flat is damp because the roof leaks. Mould grows on the walls because of the damp. The windows are never opened, partly because of traffic noise from the street outside and partly because there is a strong smell of fat from the takeaway downstairs. Gail is suffering from lack of sleep. Sometimes she hears rats under the floorboards at night. She does not let Shelley play outside because of the traffic and the large number of strangers passing by. The children have never invited any school friends home, because they are ashamed of the flat.

Gail takes her application letter along the street to the post office, where Jasmeena is behind the counter. Jasmeena sees the letter and says, 'Another application – better luck this time, maybe.'

Gail knows the lady is only trying to be friendly, but she is annoyed and snaps, 'It's none of your business, is it?'

D

Activities

Tasks 1 to 4 refer to the description of Gail Winters.

1. Identify three ways in which Gail's housing is inadequate.
2. Pick out two kinds of environmental pollution described above.
3. What problems with health and wellbeing are experienced by each member of Gail's family?
4. Which of the social factors described in Section 6.10 is causing problems for the family?
5. Which other family in Ramsay MacDonald Street probably has inadequate housing?

Activity

6 To help with revision, make up two sets of cards for the factors affecting health and wellbeing. Use different coloured card for each set. On the first set of cards, you should write the names of factors **positively** contributing to health and wellbeing. These are:

- education
- risk management
- immunisation
- stimulating work
- regular exercise
- health monitoring
- balanced diet
- health screening
- supportive relationships
- leisure
- adequate financial resources
- health promotion

On the second set of cards (on card of the other colour), you should write the names of factors **negatively** influencing health and wellbeing. These are:

- genetic diseases
- social isolation
- poverty
- unbalanced diet
- substance misuse
- inadequate housing
- unemployment
- stress
- lack of hygiene
- unprotected sex
- environmental pollution
- lack of regular exercise

On the back of each card, write a few words to remind you of things you need to know about that topic. For example on the back of the card saying 'balanced diet', you could write the names of the main food components. On the back of the card saying 'lack of regular exercise', you could list diseases related to lack of exercise. On the back of the 'unprotected sex' card, you could list the main STIs.

a Now mix the cards up and sort them into piles. One pile should be for **physical factors**, one for **economic factors**, one for **social factors** and one for **environmental factors**.

b Now mix the cards up again, and sort the cards into two groups. One group should contain the **factors that a person can control or has some control over**. The other group should be for **factors a person cannot control or has little control over**.

c Now mix the cards up again and test your memory of what is written on the back of each card. You can use this as a card game with another person.

d Mix the cards up again. Take each card and think of one thing to say about the effect of that factor on physical health and one thing to say about the effect of that factor on wellbeing.

Activity

7 Use the knowledge you have gained to predict what each of the neighbours in Ramsay MacDonald Street will be doing in 10 years' time. Each person in a group could concentrate on a different neighbour.

Then read what actually happened to them on the Nelson Thornes website.

Study tip

Try practice question 12 (page 127).

Practice questions

1. **(a)** Some students are having a discussion. Dean says, 'I know I'm healthy because I eat five portions of fruit a day and work out in the gym.' Kate replies, 'That doesn't mean you're healthy. You could have a tumour growing inside you, but not know about it.' Russell says, 'You two are always arguing. That's not healthy. There's obviously something wrong with both of you.'

    Identify and explain the definition of health which is being used by:
    - **(i)** Dean *(3 marks)*
    - **(ii)** Kate *(3 marks)*
    - **(iii)** Russell. *(3 marks)*

    (b) Using **one** example, explain how ideas of health and wellbeing can vary between different cultures. *(6 marks)*

2. Melanie is 80 years old. She takes regular exercise.
    (a) Explain **three** ways in which regular exercise can help Melanie's physical health. *(9 marks)*
    (b) Suggest **two** different ways in which regular exercise can improve Melanie's wellbeing. *(2 marks)*
    (c) Explain why physical exercise can be more difficult for a person in Melanie's life stage. *(4 marks)*

3. Nasreen is 15 years old. In a typical day, she will eat a lot of fruit, salad with oil, some rice, potatoes, bread and cakes.
    (a) Name **two** food components that are likely to be missing from Nasreen's diet and for each one suggest one food that will contain this component. *(4 marks)*
    (b) Explain why a balanced diet is important for someone at Nasreen's life stage. *(6 marks)*
    (c) Outline **one** advantage of cooking foods by steaming instead of by frying. Refer to the effects on a person's health. *(4 marks)*

4. Claire spends most evenings in a bar with her friends. On a typical night she will drink four glasses of wine and three cocktails, each containing one measure of spirits.
    (a) Explain why Claire's use of alcohol is substance misuse. *(3 marks)*
    (b) Outline the health effects on Claire of continuing to drink this amount of alcohol. *(6 marks)*

5. **(a)** Describe the main health effects on a person infected with chlamydia. *(6 marks)*
    (b) Explain how infection by chlamydia is caused. *(4 marks)*

6. Stewart has haemophilia.
    (a) Explain the possible effects of haemophilia on Stewart's health. *(3 marks)*
    (b) Outline the cause of Stewart's haemophilia. *(4 marks)*
    (c) Outline the usual treatment for haemophilia. *(2 marks)*

7 (a) Jamie is seven years old. He has asthma. Explain how the effect of asthma on Jamie's health can be monitored. *(3 marks)*

   (b) Suggest **one** different way of monitoring a person's health and explain how it can be used to prevent illness. *(6 marks)*

   (c) Using **two** different examples, explain how screening can positively contribute to a person's health. *(8 marks)*

8 Jock visits his GP. Jock is 55 years old. He has difficulty breathing and is overweight. He is a regular smoker and drinks alcohol every evening. He tells the GP that he feels tired all the time.

   (a) The GP decides to check Jock's blood pressure to see whether or not it is normal. Explain how the GP could monitor Jock's blood pressure. *(5 marks)*

   (b) The GP finds that Jock's blood pressure is 150/90. Explain whether or not this is normal. *(3 marks)*

   (c) Describe the health problems that can be caused by high blood pressure. *(8 marks)*

   (d) Suggest **one** other way in which the GP could monitor Jock's health and explain why this might be useful. *(6 marks)*

9 (a) Suggest **three** ways in which an adolescent can maintain personal hygiene. *(3 marks)*

   (b) Explain how poor personal hygiene can affect a person's health and wellbeing. *(7 marks)*

10 (a) Suggest **three** ill-health conditions that are more likely to affect poor people than better-off people. *(3 marks)*

   (b) Explain the link between poverty and ill health. *(8 marks)*

   (c) Explain why stimulating work is good for a person's health and wellbeing. *(6 marks)*

11 One social factor that can affect health and wellbeing is personal relationships.

   (a) Outline **two** other social factors that can affect health and wellbeing. *(2 marks)*

   (b) Explain how a person's relationships can affect their health and wellbeing through the life stages. *(10 marks)*

12 (a) (i) One type of environmental pollution is poor air quality. Explain the likely effects of poor air quality on a person. *(3 marks)*

       (ii) Suggest **three** other types of environmental pollution. *(3 marks)*

   (b) Explain **two** ways in which inadequate housing can negatively influence health and wellbeing. *(6 marks)*

> **Study tip** In an examination it is not easy to think up the effects of economic factors on health. You might find it useful to revise some of the PIES effects listed in this chapter using the TOP SECRET method outlined in Chapter 1 on page 16.

7 Health measures and health plans

7.1 Planning and researching Assignment 1

■ Choosing someone to study

You should first choose the person you are going to study. This might also be the person you study for Assignment 2. A suitable person is a friend or classmate. You might choose yourself, although this might be more difficult and less enjoyable.

■ Measuring physical health

You should use the following methods:

- measuring blood pressure to check the health of the circulatory system
- measuring peak flow to check the respiratory system
- measuring height and weight and calculating body mass index (BMI) to check whether the person is over- or underweight for their height
- measuring resting pulse rate, recovery pulse rate and recovery time to check the health of the circulatory system.

Read about these methods in Chapter 6, The nature of health and wellbeing, page 106 onwards.

Objectives

Explain how to use different methods of measuring health.

Measuring blood pressure

You should ensure that the person is relaxed, in a quiet environment and that you are not taking the measurement in a hurry. The person should be sitting down with their arm resting on a table. Practise using the blood pressure meter beforehand. Record the result, including the units (mmHg).

Measuring peak flow

Make sure the person is sitting down and is relaxed. Get them to hold the meter horizontally. Then ask them to take a deep breath and blow into the meter as fast and hard as they can. Repeat this three times. Each time record the result. Take the highest reading achieved. Record the result, including the units. Although the usual way of writing these units is litres per minute, you should record them as dm^3/min.

Calculating BMI

Measure the person's height without shoes. Record the height in metres (e.g. a person who is 166 centimetres tall is 1.66 metres). Weigh the person, without shoes, jacket, etc. Record the weight in kilograms (e.g. 64.5 kg).

Now square the height – i.e. multiply it by itself (e.g. 1.66 m squared = $2.7556\,m^2$). Now divide the weight by the result. (For example, divide 64.5 by 2.7556. This gives $23.40688\,kg/m^2$.)

Round this figure to one place of decimals i.e. to 23.4 kg/m². This is the person's BMI.

Measuring resting pulse rate, recovery rate and recovery time

Measure pulse rate using your fingers and a watch. Alternatively, use an electronic pulse meter. Measure pulse rate while the person is sitting down and at rest. Record this resting pulse rate in beats per minute (bpm).

A *Measuring a pulse*

Next get the person to carry out a standard exercise. A standard exercise is one that is the same for every person being tested. The ideal way to do this is to use an exercise bicycle or a gym treadmill.

Set the bicycle or treadmill at an effort level or speed that most people can manage. It must be the same for every person. Run the exercise for a standard amount of time (say, three minutes). Get the person to sit down again immediately after the exercise. One minute later, measure the pulse rate again. This is the person's recovery pulse rate. Record this in bpm. You could also keep on monitoring the pulse rate until it has returned to the resting pulse rate and record how long this took after the exercise stopped. This is recovery time.

links

www.nhsdirect.nhs.uk

www.peakflow.com

www.netdoctor.co.uk

www.netdoctor.co.uk/health_advice

Activities

1. Collect the results of these measures for all the people in your class. Try to explain why different people have got different results. Discuss what they tell you about fitness levels.
2. For the pulse rate measures, work out the mean rates for the whole class. This will be useful when you write Assignment 1.
3. You might find it useful to process the data in other ways too.
   a. You could find the mean blood pressure of the smokers and the non-smokers.
   b. You could compare people who take regular exercise with those who take little or no exercise.

   These data will be useful for Assignment 2.

7.2 Planning and researching Assignment 2

Assignment 2 requires you to focus on one individual. There are some advantages in studying the same individual as you did for Assignment 1, although you do not have to. You could choose to study yourself, although the task is likely to be more interesting and meaningful if you study a friend or classmate.

The assignment is about making recommendations for improving the individual's health.

You should choose any three from the following factors affecting physical health:

- diet
- exercise
- relationships
- substance use
- work, education and leisure.

When making your choice, you might think about which of these will be easiest to investigate. You should also try to choose the factors you are interested in yourself. You will find information on these factors in Chapter 6, The nature of health and wellbeing.

Objectives
Research areas for improving health.

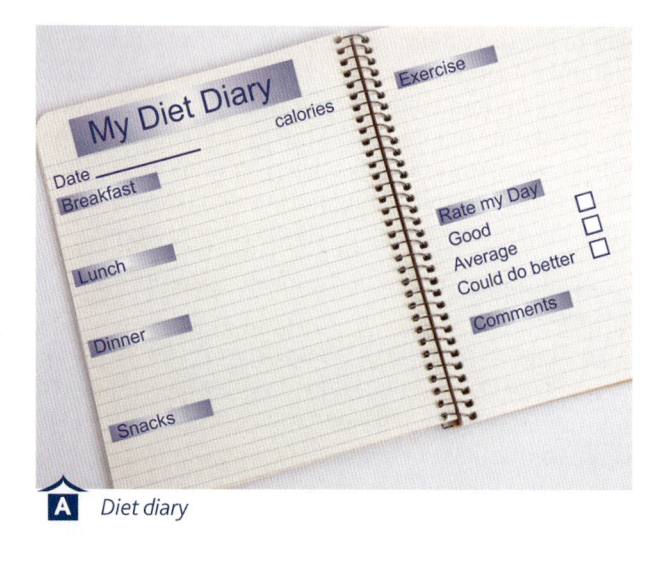

Collecting data about the person

You should collect information about the person's lifestyle, depending on which factors you have chosen. You should use several different methods of data collection, including:

- diaries (e.g. of food or alcohol consumption)
- interviews
- observations of the person.

Diaries

You might ask the person to make a note of everything they eat over a typical period, such as a few days or a week. If possible, the weight of each food eaten should be recorded. The person could make a note of how many cigarettes they smoke over a similar period.

Collect these diaries. It does not matter if they are untidy or on odd scraps of paper. They should be kept for inclusion in the Appendix.

A Diet diary

Interviews

You should also ask the person questions, and note down their answers. Once again, these data should be kept for the Appendix. Note that it would not be ethical for you to ask a person about illegal drug use. If you have chosen substance abuse, you should only ask about legal substances.

Observations

Everyday observations can also be useful. For example, you can get an impression of a person's diet and how much physical activity they do by spending time with them. Keep your notes.

Collecting information from other sources

You should also collect information from sources that will help you to analyse what you have found out about the person you studied.

For example, you should find sources of information about the food components and calories present in various foods in the person's diet. Some packaged foods give very detailed information. For example a 420 g tin of baked beans gives the weight of each food component in a 210 g serving (i.e. half a tin). This tells you that the total food energy content is 166 kilocalories, and that food components include 10.5 g of protein, 29.2 g of carbohydrate and 11.3 g of fibre. There are several websites that help you to calculate the contents of a diet. (Note: these are commercial companies that might be trying to sell you a diet.)

B *Some packaged foods give detailed information on food components*

You might also find information about the number of units of alcohol in the drinks recorded in the alcohol diary.

You should also look for health-promotion materials that relate to the factors you have chosen. These might include leaflets and websites. A small number of leaflets or single pages from websites can be put in an Appendix. Keep a note of the names of any websites found.

links

www.weightlossresources.co.uk

Ridgwell Press produces a CD-ROM called 'Food in Focus' which allows you to find out the nutritional content of a person's diet.

links

www.nhs.uk/units

www.drinkaware.co.uk

www.lookoutalcohol.co.uk

links

www.gosmokefree.nhs.uk

www.canstopsmoking.com

www.nhsdirect.nhs.uk/magazine/interactive/calories/index.aspx

Index

A
Abuse 38
Access to services 62
Action slips 24
Acute (hospital) trusts 67
Addiction 92–93
Adolescence 16–19
Adolescent growth spurt 16
Adulthood 20–21
Age Concern 33
AIDS 97
Alcoholism 93
Anaemia 47
Anti-discriminatory practice 74–75
Attachment 12
Autism 45
Autonomy 15

B
Bacteria 49, 99
Balanced diet 89
Barriers to access 62–63
Bereavement 25
Binge drinking 93
Blood pressure 83–84, 106
Blood testing 106
Body image 18
Body mass index (BMI) 109
Bonding 12
Bronchitis 92

C
Calories 47
Cancer 49
Carbohydrates 47
Care actions 65
Care providers 74
Care skills 68–72
Cervical cancer 99, 105
Childhood 14–15
ChildLine 34
Chlamydia 98
Cholesterol 47, 84
Chromosomes 46
Circulatory system 83
Cirrhosis 93
Citizen's Advice Bureau 33
Code of practice (conduct) 75, 77
Colour blindness 101
Communication 69–70
Community nurse 33
Conception 45
Concepts 9
Confidentiality 75
Cooperation 9
Coronary artery disease 84
Counselling 71
Curiosity 14
Cultural barrier 63
Culture 43

D
Data interpretation 68
Definitions of health and wellbeing 78–79
Development: types of 8–9
Developmental assessment 13, 72
Diabetes 48, 86
Diagnosis 69
Diastolic blood pressure 107
Diet 46–48, 88–91
Discrimination 74
Distraction 71
District nurse 33
DNA 45
Down's syndrome 45, 102

E
Emotional abuse 39
Emotional development 9
Empathy 15
Employment contract 75
Environmental factors 122
Ethnicity 43
Exercise 83–87
Expected and unexpected events 29

F
Factors affecting self-concept 43–44
Factors in life 45–52
Faith-based services 33–34
Family relationships 36
Fats 47
Fibre 46
Financial barrier 63
Financial resources 114
Fine motor skills 8
Flexibility 24
Food components 46–48
Formal support 33
Four humour theory 80
Friendships 36

G
General practitioner (GP) 33
Genes 45
Genetically inherited diseases 100–103
Genetic factors 100
Genetic inheritance 45, 49
Genital warts 99
Geographical barrier 63
Germ theory 80
Gonorrhoea 98
Gross motor skills 8
Growth 8

H
Haemophilia 45
Health and safety 74
Health care assistant 33
Health monitoring 106–109
Health plan 131
Health promotion 110
Heart attack 84
Heart disease 84
Heart failure 84
Heel-prick test 105
Herpes 98

Index

HIV/AIDS 97
Holistic definition (of health and wellbeing) 79
Home care assistant 33
Hot flushes 20
Housing conditions 51, 122
HPV (Human papilloma virus) 99
Huntington's disease 101
Hygiene 112–113
Hypertension 84
Hypothermia 51

I

Illness prevention 104
Impairments 65
Immune system 105
Immunisation 105
Impotence 20
Income 50
Incontinence 113
Independence 15, 74
Individual differences 45
Infancy 10–13
Infant mortality 114
Informal support 32
Insulin 87
Integrated services 61
Intellectual development 9
Intimate, personal and sexual relationships 36

K

Kilocalories 46

L

Lack of support 39
Language barrier 63
Later adulthood 24–25
Leadership 72
Learning impairment 65
Leisure 117
Life events 28–31
Life stages 8
Lifestyle factors 115
Lung cancer 92
Lung function 85

M

Mammogram 105
Material possessions 50
Memory 24
Menopause 20
Menstruation 16
Methods of referral 62
Microorganisms 80
Milk teeth 10
Mineral 47
Mobility 8, 83
Modelling 71
Monitoring 73
Mood swings 18
Motor development 8
Motor milestones 11

N

National Health Service (NHS) 60
Needs 51, 58–59
Needs assessment 71
Neglect 39
Night sweats 20
Non-verbal communication 78
NSP 47

O

Obesity 49
Observation 68
Occupational therapist 33
Oestrogen 16, 20
Osteoporosis 83, 87
Ovulation 16, 20

P

Partnership working 61
Peak flow 110
Peers 18, 36
Permanent teeth 14
Personal hygiene 112–113
Physical abuse 39
Physical activity 49
Physical barrier 63
Physical development 8
Physical factors 79, 83
Physical impairment 65

Physiotherapist 33
PKU 101
Policies 75
Pollution 51–52
Poor-quality diet 49
Postcode lottery 52
Poverty 94, 114–115
Primary care trusts 61
Primary health care 59
Principles of care 74–75
Private sector 59–60
Professional carers 33
Professional referral 62
Progesterone 16, 20
Protein 47
Psychological abuse 39
Psychological barrier 63
Puberty 16–17
Pulse rate 83, 107

R

Radioactivity 123
Reaction time 24
Recovery pulse rate 108
Recovery time 108
Redundancy 28
Rehabilitation 64
Relate 33
Relationships 36–37, 118–119
Resource barrier 63
Respiratory system 85
Resting pulse rate 107
Retirement 25, 28
Risk assessment 109
Risk management 109
Romantic relationships 19

S

Samaritans 34
Screening 105
Secondary health care 59
Secondary sexual characteristics 17
Self-concept 43
Self-confidence 12
Self-consciousness 18
Self-esteem 18

Self-referral	62	Stamina	85	**U**		
Sensory impairment	65	Statutory sector	59–60	Unemployment	116	
Service aims	64	Stress	120–122	**V**		
Setting challenges	71	Stressor	120	Vaccination	105	
Sex chromosomes	102	Stress test	108	Verbal communication	69	
Sex hormones	16	Stroke	84	Virus	48, 97	
Sexual abuse	39	Substance misuse	94–95	Vitamins	47	
Sexually transmitted infection (STI)	97–99	Supportive relationships	118	Vocabulary	14	
Shamanism	80	Support staff	77	Voluntary sector	59–60	
Smear test	105	Systolic blood pressure	107	Voluntary services	33–34	
Social and environmental factors	117–125	**T**		**W**		
Social awkwardness	19	Tantrums	12	Wants	52	
Social development	9	Teamworking	72	Weight control	85	
Social interactions	9	Temperature	106	Wisdom	25	
Social isolation	25, 120	Testosterone	16	Work	115–116	
Social worker	33	Thermometer	106	Working relationships	36	
Solvents	95	Third-party referral	62			
Sources of support	32–35	Tobacco	92			
Sphygmomanometer	107	Treatment	69			